off-script

a mom's journey through adoption,
a husband's alcoholism,
and special needs parenting

valerie cantella

Recovering Perfectionist Press

Published in Santa Barbara California, by Recovering Perfectionist Press.
www.ValerieCantella.com

ISBN (paperback): 979-8-9851847-0-9
ISBN (eBook): 979-8-9851847-1-6
Library of Congress Control Number 2021923849

We are unreliable narrators of our own stories
and I share this memoir with that caveat.
There may be other versions of these events,
but this is my heartfelt recollection of my experiences.

Chapter One

Don't judge my story by the chapter you walked in on.

Unknown

Angry storm clouds, pregnant with rain, screamed with lightning as I gripped the seat handles and stared out the window of the plane, willing this trip to Montana to be over. The dark, tumultuous sky seemed to mirror our family's last two and a half months. I gazed at my thirteen-year-old daughter, Katie, as she clutched her pillow pet, Steve, her fingers white from the pressure. She shifted in her seat and chewed a fingernail, already red and irritated, gnawed to the bone. I gently pushed her fingers from her mouth, so she tugged on her hair instead. I cringed at the bald patch on her scalp and decided to let her be for the moment. This wasn't a battle worth fighting this evening.

A flash of lightning caused her to yelp, so I slammed the window shade shut, wishing it would seal us off from life, and resisted pulling her to me. When I tentatively put my hand on her shoulder, she shrugged it away, a mixture of anger and fear in her eyes. She hugged Steve's colorless body, worn with love and age, tighter and buried her head in him.

Katie couldn't be comforted. As an adopted child with reactive attachment disorder, she didn't like to be touched. She wasn't like her brother, Nick, older by eighteen months and our only biological child. As a toddler, he loved to snuggle while I read to him, and at fourteen, he still occasionally asked me to rub his back. But she never asked for anything, and it seemed nothing made her comfortable. Katie was suffering, and we were out of options.

The perky flight attendant, in her crisp navy uniform, strapped in across from us, mouthed, "Is there anything you need?"

I automatically smiled and shook my head, then rested my head against the side of the plane. There was so much I needed, but nothing a polished stranger could help with. It was nearly one a.m., and I knew the day ahead would suck every ounce of energy from me. Between the turbulence of the summer sky and Katie's emotional rollercoaster, a few hours of sleep were the best we could hope for.

The last twenty-four hours at our home in Santa Barbara had been excruciating. Katie halfheartedly threw things and cried, "I want to die" and "Can you please just kill me?" She moaned and snarled like an animal ready to pounce, then fell to the floor, sobbing. Nick watched, then frowned and pushed his shaggy brown hair out of his eyes, grabbed his skateboard, and left to be with his friends. I wished I could do that, too, but as the mom, I had to keep it together.

Shortly after that, my husband joined Katie and me as we left for the airport. Because it was a last-minute trip scheduled in desperation, we'd gotten the seats from Los Angeles, California, to Billings, Montana, but they weren't together. With the turbulence, I wished my husband was sitting with us. He thought he was generous by giving the first-class seats to Katie and me. But it was more likely because of our respective roles. As the mom, I was the primary caregiver and "keeper-together" of the household. Like many moms, I took the kids to school, kept track of the permission slips and grades, provided homemade treats for class parties, helped with homework, grocery shopped and cleaned, managed doctor and dentist appointments, and comforted them when they were sad or sick. Dad, well, he went to work, and when he was at home, he was just there, often passed out on the couch after dinner and a few martinis.

We finally landed at two a.m. and, uncharacteristically, Katie fell asleep almost immediately. Later that morning, we visited a local bakery for a giant, world-famous cinnamon roll before taking Katie to her new home, a residential treatment center where she would live for an unknown amount of time.

Paul and I tried to make small talk with her, but it felt like conversing with a death-row inmate before their execution. *What was there to say?*

We arrived early for the check-in and wandered around the lush green campus under an expansive blue sky with fluffy clouds. A sense of peace and serenity filled the air that smelled of fresh-cut grass. We encountered a pile of rocks and a sign describing a school tradition in which graduating students picked a stone to commemorate their journey and remember the lessons learned. It gave us hope Katie could recover.

A staff member greeted us warmly and invited us into a conference room with an old wooden table surrounded by dated blue upholstered chairs with rounded edges. The treatment team included a case manager, dietician, nurse, therapist, doctor, psychiatrist, and admissions manager. They were all gathered to meet our family and admit Katie to the facility.

After giving a brief introduction of each team member and an overview of the program, the case manager started asking his list of questions, including Katie's name, date of birth, address, parents, siblings, emergency contact information, primary language, household size, and marital status. The warm air felt stifling, and I thought I might be sick.

I exhaled loudly. "Is this really necessary? I sent all the documents over last week."

The case manager explained they wanted to hear the information from us. Paul and I slumped in our chairs as seven pairs of eyes waited expectantly for our responses. "Religious affiliation?"

"Christian," I replied.

"Current legal status?"

I paused. "I'm not sure what you mean. We legally adopted her from Russia, and she is a U.S. citizen. Here are her U.S. and Russian passports," I said as I slid them across the table.

"Great," the case manager said. "But we're really looking for whether she's been involved with law enforcement or the courts."

"Oh … no," I replied, embarrassed I misunderstood the question.

"Approved contacts?"

"Approved contacts?" I asked, not wanting to misunderstand the question again.

"It's a list of people who are allowed to call, write, or visit Catherine."

My face tightened, annoyed they called her by her formal name when I told them she went by Katie.

"Oh," I replied and looked at Paul. "Us, her brother, her grandparents, her aunt, and uncle…"

Then the psychiatrist inquired about the problems which brought us to the school.

"Most of it's in the fifty pages of documents," I said sharply.

"It would be good for us to hear directly from you," he replied gently

My stomach clenched, and I took a breath. Katie was sitting next to me. It felt so impersonal and awkward to be answering these questions in front of her. But she wasn't going to respond, so I started listing things off. "She ran away and is anxious and depressed. She's having suicidal ideations and allegedly tried once."

The therapist nodded. "Self-injurious behaviors?"

"She's been pulling out her hair, if that's what you mean, and I think done some cutting," I replied as I glanced at her medium-length, mushroom brown hair and the spot where there was none. Her tattered burgundy sweatshirt and faded jeans covered any indication she'd been cutting recently.

His list of questions continued—physical or verbal aggression, fire setting, animal cruelty, stealing, destructive behaviors, impulsive, sexualized behaviors, physical abuse, difficulties with authority?

"No, no, no, no, no."

"Hallucinations or paranoia?"

"Not that I know of," I replied.

"Is she non-verbal?"

We all turned toward Katie, who had her head resting on the table. She didn't respond, and I didn't know if she was ignoring us or checked out. I started to say something to her and thought better of it.

"No," I replied.

"Self-care skill needs?"

"Yes."

"Can you describe those?"

"Right now, she barely gets out of bed. We have to force her to eat and shower. She knows how to dress and brush her teeth ... is that what you want to know?" I asked.

He nodded. "Current diagnoses?"

Oh, where to start. "Reactive attachment disorder, anxiety, depression, sensory integration issues, and fetal alcohol syndrome." I glanced over at Paul. "Did I miss Anything?"

He shook his head and said, "None that I can think of."

"Current medications?"

I pulled a list from our binder and handed it to the doctor.

"Previous placements?"

"None."

The case manager asked about Katie's family history.

"We adopted her from Russia at sixteen months old. She was only fifteen pounds and severely malnourished. You could see every bone in her body ..." my voice trailed off, not wanting to discuss it in front of Katie. While she knew she was adopted, she had never wanted any information about the orphanage or her birth mother, and we never offered any.

After what seemed like hours, we stood up and stretched. The team invited us to tour the campus. The well-used school was cozier than the junior high at home, and the horse arena where they did equine therapy piqued Katie's interest momentarily. A church filled one corner of the property and offered Wednesday night youth groups and Sunday services. Welcome signs and encouraging notes decorated the single-story, brick, ranch-style lodge where Katie would live. Her new housemates were boisterous and chatty, excited to meet Katie. As we said goodbye, the warm chaplain with his ruddy, Santa-like face prayed over our family.

As the case manager walked Paul and me to the car, he said, "Take a week off, Valerie. You have done so much. Don't feel guilty, you didn't cause this."

Words could not adequately describe the emotions surrounding that day. Paul and I were numb but grateful; sad but relieved Katie would be safe under someone else's watch. We were utterly depleted.

After leaving the campus, Paul and I drove a meandering road showcasing Montana's gorgeous mountains, enormous hats, and endless blue skies. It soothed us as we tried to leave behind the trauma of the previous months. We returned to Santa Barbara to figure out what life without Katie would be like.

Chapter Two

When you go through deep waters, I'll be with you.

Isaiah 432

The ten weeks before we dropped Katie off in Montana had been excruciating. My mind wandered back to April when everything had suddenly changed. I had just returned from a week of advanced public information training with FEMA/Homeland Security. The professional development was engaging and demanding, but also rewarding. Adrenaline coursed through my body when the instructors selected me over twenty-six others to lead the final two-day emergency exercise. Our team performed well. The accolades and respect provided a welcome contrast to the inadequacy I felt in parenting Katie. As we headed home, our instructors noted it was typical for someone from the class to experience an incident within a few months. I never suspected it would be me.

A week after I returned, my cell phone rang with an automated call from the junior high, noting they had marked Katie absent. The message asked me to call back to confirm the reason for the absence. *That's weird. I thought Katie rode her bike to school today.*

"Hi, it's Valerie, Katie's mom, calling you back," I casually said while flipping through some papers on my desk.

"Oh, hi Valerie," said the friendly office assistant. "We just wanted to find out if Katie was sick today."

My brow furled. "No, she rode her bike this morning," I replied. "Are you sure she isn't there?"

"No, we had one of the staff look in all the places students hide but didn't see her."

"That's weird … hmm. I'll be right over to see if her bike is there."

She should have been in class, but I tried her cell phone, anyway. It went to voicemail, and I hung up.

I texted Paul. "Did you see Katie leave for school?"

"Yes," he promptly replied.

"She's not there … they can't find her."

He called me, and I relayed the conversation with the attendance clerk. I suggested we check our house and her likely route to school. He agreed with that plan and headed to the park she rode through. I rushed out of my office to drive home. She wasn't there, but her cell phone sat on her dresser.

My brain couldn't put the pieces together. *Where was Katie?*

Pulling out my phone, I dialed a colleague who was a deputy sheriff.

"Hi, it's Valerie," I said abruptly, trying to avoid small talk.

"Hi Valerie, how are you?" he asked in a warm and friendly tone.

"I'm okay, but listen, I need some help," I replied as I stood out on the street, looking up to see if Katie was around.

"What can I do?" he asked, calm but concerned.

"My daughter, Katie, didn't show up at school today … my husband saw her leave on her bike, but she's not at our house, and he's checking the park she would have ridden through," I explained.

"I don't know what the situation at home is, but I have to ask, is it possible she's run away?" he gently asked.

Speechless, I paused. "Katie has significant special needs … she's kind of like an autistic kid. I don't know where she would run to."

Where *would* she go? She didn't have any friends, and I didn't think she would walk to my parents' house, which was close to her school. They would have called me, but I called them anyway, and asked them to pray. The idea of her running away made little sense, but running away sounded better than an abduction

Five minutes later, I arrived at the school. Paul stood as stiff and straight as a flagpole, his face pale as he spoke with a deputy. As I ran up the steps, the deputy turned toward me, raising his eyebrows and questioning why I was there. It wasn't an incident that required me to be there in my professional capacity as the City's public information officer.

"I'm the mom," I quickly explained.

Emergencies brought out the best in me. My natural focus and composure allowed me to complete tasks in logical, sequential order with little emotion. Then, when I had time to reflect on what could have been, tears fell uncontrollably. That day was no different. It felt like an out-of-body experience—the professional me observing the mother in a personal crisis, with the detached professional winning out.

As Paul and I walked into the school office, the school staff offered small, sympathetic smiles. The cantankerous principal greeted us in a voice too cheery for the circumstances. She showed no empathy or support, and it felt like a slap across the face after all the time and energy I'd spent volunteering there.

Two deputies peppered us with questions we answered as best we could, but we were at a complete loss. When they asked if there had been problems at home. I said she was isolated and withdrawn, but this was not new behavior.

I stepped out to call Nick, grateful he was on lunch break and could answer.

"What's up?" he asked.

"Has Katie told you anything about being unhappy at home?"

"What? No," he said. "Why?"

I didn't know how to continue. There was no easy way to say it.

"Katie didn't show up for school today, and we can't find her or her bike," I replied.

"What?" He murmured some distressed noises and said, "Can I help look for her?"

"Yes, of course," I hurriedly blurted. "I've got to go talk to the deputies. I'll call you back in a minute."

Just as the deputies left to search for her, Paul's phone rang.

"Is this Katie's father?" a female voice asked.

"Yes," he replied and put his phone on speaker so we could all listen in.

"We have Katie, and she's safe," said an unidentified woman who identified herself as staff from a safe house for abused youth in Santa Barbara we had never heard of. "Katie took the bus here today and will stay with us for a while, but we'd like to invite you and Katie's mother to come down for a family session this afternoon."

Our confusion and relief grew simultaneously—at least she was safe. *But how had Katie figured this out?* She couldn't remember the names of our friends and neighbors or have a regular conversation that included multiple sentences or exchanges of information. She'd never used money to buy anything and didn't know how to count coins. The most leeway we'd given her was riding to school. Even that one and a quarter-mile trip was simple—a straight line from our house to the junior high through a neighborhood park. How had Katie gotten on a public bus with a backpack full of clothes and bus fare without her phone? She'd never taken public transportation alone, yet, somehow, she transferred buses at least once, then walked from the transfer station to an unmarked home. Katie memorized the details—the bus schedule and route, the address, and their sequencing. As soon as I realized this, I wondered if she had been fooling us all along.

One of Katie's classmates had run away to this same shelter when her mother had burned her with cigarettes for getting poor grades. In Katie's limited understanding and deep despair, she thought running away to this shelter would help her, too. Her peer described the exact details of what to do, what to say, and what to pack. Katie committed this to memory and planned her actions.

While the hour or two she was missing were excruciating, we learned she had a greater capacity than we'd ever observed. If there had to be a silver lining, that was it. But had she manipulated us, something common for children with reactive attachment disorder? It felt awful even to consider a child being devious, but it made sense, based on a book I'd read years earlier—one about children without a conscience. Maybe Katie felt in control when she said, "I don't know." It made us think she didn't know. Instead, I questioned whether she just didn't want to answer. *Could I trust her, or did I have to second guess everything she said now?*

I picked Nick up from the high school, explaining Katie was safe and the little information I knew. He shared my confusion. The Katie we knew barely got to school, rarely spoke unless spoken to, and preferred to be unseen. Could a girl like her really do all she had?

Thousands of thoughts and questions churned in my head. When Paul and I met with Katie and the staff member that evening, we realized the depth of Katie's anxiety and depression. She described the bullying at school, which caused her to scratch at her wrists until they bled, and she explained feeling weak and dizzy each day. But instead of asking us or anyone else for help, she figured running away would get our attention. It did.

The night after she ran away, I led a school board meeting but felt like such a fraud. Our superintendent knew what had happened, but none of my colleagues were aware. How could I lead the school board when my daughter had just run away? How could I have not seen the anxiety and depression which made her think running away was the answer? It was undoubtedly my fault. If I had only done better, known better, and been a better Christian, this would not have happened.

The following days ran together like wet paint dripped on a canvas. After a few days at the shelter, we brought her back home. Fear gripped my soul, and my eyes felt like sandpaper every time I blinked. My neck and shoulders were like a granite slab. How were we going to survive this?

Chapter Three

Pray as though everything depended on God.
Work as though everything depended on you.

Saint Augustine

Life turned into two distinct chapters—the days before Katie ran away from home and the days after. We were not a happy family of four before, though we refused to acknowledge it and take action. But afterward, we could no longer ignore the dysfunction in front of us. Paul and I could never understand the depth of Katie's pain and feared she might harm herself or run away again.

Church was an essential part of our lives, and we relied on the small group we met with weekly for support and comfort. They knew some of our family's challenges, but we decided to share a request with the church's prayer chain after Katie ran away. It was uncomfortable to put things out in the world because of the attention it would bring. I certainly didn't want people to know how bad our lives had become. When we previously shared our struggles with Katie, people didn't believe us, so I feared they would think we were overly dramatic now. But we had to do something. Our situation was so terrible, Paul and I eventually agreed to share this with the church prayer chain.

> Our daughter Katie was severely depressed and ran away to a shelter a few weeks ago. It was a wake-up call for us. We are seeking guidance on how to treat her depression and attempting to find the right therapist to help the four of us deal with her Asperger's syndrome, reactive attachment disorder, and obsessive-compulsive disorder. We are also working with the school to expand her supports

People prayed and sympathized. But no one truly understood the magnitude of her problems and our confusion in untangling the mess. Holding everything together became too much. Running until my legs screamed and listening to angry music at loud volumes helped dissolve the anger I felt at being helpless. I allowed myself five minutes of pity a day but pushed forward afterward. Paul's coping mechanism was alcohol. Nick escaped our high-strung household and hung out with friends. The crumbling of the facade had begun.

A few weeks later, Katie was working with the therapist from the shelter, while I sat in the waiting room on a lumpy futon in a sunny office. She and the therapist mostly drew pictures and played games. Katie didn't have the emotional and intellectual capacity to take part in talk therapy

Can this really be helping? I thought, looking at my watch. Nick was surfing, and I needed to pick him up. Paul was halfway to China for work, so I was a single parent for the week.

Katie's therapist came out to say Katie was expressing suicidal ideations. The therapist couldn't decide if Katie was planning to harm herself or simply making statements to get attention.

Why are you asking me? What did I know? I hadn't seen Katie's huge meltdown coming, so I certainly wasn't reliable now. After a half-hour of back and forth, I took Katie to the emergency room, where the doctor placed her on an involuntary psychiatric hold for 72-hours.

With Paul on a plane, I didn't know whether to text him. It would be a disturbing message to receive upon arrival at the Beijing Airport on top of an already taxing trip. He was there to solve a problem with a vendor or a client. I couldn't remember. He was often the fixer for his company, and he could do nothing to help with this from thousands of miles away. So, I decided against telling him because when he was stressed, I felt stressed, and I didn't need any on my plate.

My parents came over to sit with me while I waited for information and guidance from the emergency room personnel. Katie slept for hours under the watchful eye of a guard, but didn't receive treatment. In the middle of the night, a therapist came from some organization to evaluate her. He said he would look for a bed for her. Having no experience with psychiatric holds, I didn't know this meant his team would look for a space at an adolescent psychiatric facility. Exhausted, I drove home and tried to sleep.

The next day was Goleta's annual State of the City event. Scripting speeches and creating presentations for our City Manager and elected officials was my responsibility. So I already felt pressure without Katie's situation in the mix. As I stood in my beautiful red suit surveying the hotel ballroom, set for the crowd of several hundred business and community leaders, I felt a sense of control and confidence. It was a stark contrast to the bleak hospital room where I felt inadequate and lost.

After the event, I went back to the hospital, the second day of Katie's stay. The nurse told me "they" were searching for an adolescent psychiatric facility with an available bed for Katie, but I didn't know who "they" were or how long the hospital would hold Katie. The snails' pace and the lack of communication frustrated me. I didn't know what to do or expect and the hours ticked by with little movement. I certainly wasn't prepared to have her back at home if she continued to be suicidal.

On the third day of her hospitalization, safety planning for her release began. There were no available beds at any psychiatric facility serving youth in southern California. I realized if I didn't pull together a plan that worked for me, they would send home Katie with no support for her or me. Katie's psychiatrist, our family therapist, the youth facility staff, my parents, and I created a temporary emergency plan for her next few days.

She left the hospital, and I took her to the youth shelter until Paul returned. Then we'd reevaluate the situation.

Two days later, my phone rang, and the caller ID displayed the shelter's name. The voice on the other end asked if I was Katie's mom. When I said I was, she immediately announced Katie tried to hang herself.

"What?" I stammered into the phone.

"Katie reported she tried to hang herself last night. There were no marks on her neck, and we're not sure what happened. She was in her room alone."

"So, she didn't actually try? She just reported that she tried?"

"Yes, we called the crisis line, and they talked to her."

Oh. My. Lord. I was new to the trauma arena, but that was no way to start a conversation. *Why hadn't they called me twelve hours earlier when it happened? Was I the enemy? What was the crisis line?* (It turned out it was a mobile response team trained to help youth in crisis.)

Life with Katie had always been challenging, but the weeks after she ran away were excruciating. Nick was heartbroken for Katie, although he couldn't express it. He tried to hold it together for us because he saw how stressed we were. With all my focus on Katie, I neglected to offer space for him to talk through his feelings.

Bizarre emails to her teacher and dark drawings and notes scribbled on tiny pieces of paper scattered about her room spoke to her demise. One email to her teacher said, "I guess you don't have a heart." Another said, "Goodbye."

It wasn't a complete surprise. Katie had seen a psychiatrist six months earlier because she seemed more withdrawn and moody than usual. Because she couldn't verbalize her feelings, we didn't set up regular sessions, so we then tried medication. The medications caused her to sleep eighteen to twenty hours a day, with no improvement in her mood for the few hours she was awake. That didn't feel healthy, and not knowing that it took six weeks for them to kick in, we had her stop taking them. In retrospect, we wondered if we made the right decision—if we should have kept her on them. Sleeping was better than dying.

Working with the school to amend the individualized education plan (IEP) we'd agreed upon a few months earlier was challenging. At that time, Katie had been passing her classes, which meant she was doing well. A plan for support in high school had been put in place. But everything had changed by her running away and we pushed for another meeting. They claimed to not have time. Katie hadn't been at school more than a few days over the past month, and so it wasn't a problem that was right in front of them. This actually worked in our favor because the truancy triggered a mandatory meeting to discuss what support they would offer. The school psychiatrist said Katie did not qualify for social-emotional supports because she was doing well in her classes. But that woman later admitted to never reading Katie's file. We demanded new IEP testing since the team ignored her social-emotional needs, and they agreed. They also decided she had enough credits to pass eighth grade, without attending class or doing any work. Katie barely got out of bed, and when she did, she looked like a street urchin with her wild, uncombed hair, her unnaturally pale face, and unpleasant body odor. She hardly ate and only changed out of her beloved green sweatshirt and black yoga pants when the smell was so bad it was no longer tolerable. The school district team agreed to reconvene a few weeks later, after they'd completed additional testing. Given Katie's low level of functioning, I didn't know how successful that would be, but it was worth a shot.

At home, Katie vacillated between sobbing and raging. Sometimes she sat blank-faced over her food at the kitchen island, catatonic. One minute she played her Nintendo DS, and the next, she was throwing a tantrum. She moaned and cried, "I think I'm going to die soon. I don't know how much time I have left," and "I'm dying slowly." Paul, Nick, and I didn't know how to react, so we walked on eggshells, afraid of her and her reactions.

Everything felt unbearable and arduous. Even the simplest tasks frustrated me. Researching options for our next steps became my primary focus on top of my full-time job. My eyes burned, my head ached, and my heart was heavy as I realized that some sort of residential program was the most suitable option for Katie in her current state. Yet, moving a child with reactive attachment disorder to a new living situation with a different caregiver was contrary to everything I'd ever heard from doctors or read about appropriate treatment. But Paul and I felt we had no other choice, given her profound needs.

Night after night, I pored over various program options, doing endless internet searches, emailing with other parents and providers. Life felt like one of those little plastic puzzles where you move the tiles around to get the numbers to add up. One piece just needed to be solidified so we could move the other parts into place. I struggled with knowing when to push and when to back off, believing God would move the pieces into place at the right time. Yet I couldn't understand why God wasn't clearing the path. I was in a pressure cooker, trying to find the relief valve. What would happen to our family if I melted down, too?

It was seven weeks after Katie ran away that Paul and I concluded we needed to move her into residential treatment. We couldn't keep her at home because of the chaos and stress it put on the four of us, not to mention that it wasn't helping Katie, our highest priority. During the time we were weighing our options, my parents watched Katie in their home for over a week to monitor her while we worked. Knives, medications, scissors, sewing implements, tools, and anything that could be used for self-harm got locked away. She screamed and threatened suicide. When they'd reached their limit, fearful she might harm herself, they called us to pick her up. Soon after that, my parents asked for our forgiveness for the years they thought we were exaggerating. They'd finally experienced it for themselves.

About this time, I flew to Montana to tour a potential treatment facility for Katie. Paul had returned the previous evening from visiting one in Colorado. Strict rules and high cost of land in California seemed to push these schools into states like Montana, Utah, and Texas. Deciding to send Katie out of state for an unknown amount of time felt significant and painful. *How would we make the right decision? Was it the right decision? If it worked out, it was God's will, right?*

Montana was under an extreme weather warning when I arrived. The dude-ranch hotel's welcome package included directions to the tornado shelter from my room with knotty pine walls and exposed beams. It brought me back to those humid summer days in Illinois when my friends and I sang songs and waited for the inevitable downpour and tornado warning. The newscaster's voice boomed in my head. *"Today, conditions are ripe for tornados and severe weather, and NOAA has issued a tornado watch. Prepare now and be ready to take immediate action."*

During the previous two months, it felt like massive, destructive tornadoes had come at our family, one right after the other. I couldn't even catch my breath to prepare myself for the next one. My body was stiff, always bracing for the next twist. Details crammed my brain, which constantly sorted and filtered through them, trying to figure out a plan. I was sheltering in place, protecting my head and heart fiercely, and hoping my entire life would not uproot like Auntie Em's house in the *Wizard of Oz*.

The tornado warning paralyzed me. Even though it was unlikely it would come by my hotel, on that street, on that night, I couldn't sleep. My mind filtered through the worst-case scenarios for both the weather and Katie's situation. Thankfully, no tornados hit that evening. The tour was informative and gave me peace about sending Katie there

When I returned home, as expected, the meeting with the school district did not go well. Their twenty-four-page report confirmed Katie's severe anxiety and depression, and it was horrifying to read she was in the 99th percentile for depression on most tests. We had removed Katie from the most stressful school environment, and her emotional state decayed even further despite multiple support and therapy appointments each week, along with medication. Their response to this was just four hours per day of summer school for three and a half weeks. It was woefully inadequate. And just wouldn't cut it.

I tried to reason with them and asked, "How is taking part in a summer school program, which would require Katie to get up early and have some level of personal hygiene appropriate?"

While the report was heartbreaking, it also confirmed we were doing the right thing for her health and safety. Paul and I knew she was in serious trouble and would soon become a statistic if we couldn't find her intensive help. The school district wouldn't approve a residential placement for Katie because they needed to show other interventions were unsuccessful first. Under normal circumstances, this was reasonable, but Katie was ready to jump off the cliff, and we couldn't take that chance. She was barely hanging on.

Trying to show the dire nature of the situation, I sent the district six videos of Katie in distress. One of them, taken in our kitchen, showed her whimpering and moaning. *"Why am I not dead?"* She bit into a plum and immediately tossed it in the trash. *"Ohhh, that's going to kill me. Am I having a heart attack ... I don't know what a heart attack is, but I think I might get one. I wish I could just eat ... when I eat, I might suffocate myself. Everything hurts ... can you make me pass out?"*

If that didn't help them understand, I didn't know what would. I clung to the belief God could work miracles. My life verse from junior high came back to me.

Jeremiah 29:11-13: *"For I know the plans I have for you," declares the Lord, "plans to prosper you and not to harm you, plans to give you hope and a future. Then you will call on me and come and pray to me, and I will listen to you. You will seek me and find me when you seek me with all your heart."*

The residential treatment center accepted her, and we felt confident it was the best option for all of us. We also felt we had no other choice.

Chapter Four

Rest with Me a while. You have journeyed up a steep, rugged path in recent days. The way ahead is shrouded in uncertainty. Look neither behind you nor before you. Instead, focus your attention on Me, your Companion. Trust that I will equip you fully for whatever awaits you on your journey …

Sarah Young, *Jesus Calling*

After dropping Katie off at the residential treatment facility in Montana, Paul and I enjoyed an evening with no conversation about her for the first time in two and a half months. It had been a week without Katie, and we relished the respite from the feeling the sky was falling. Katie's case manager called at 8 p.m., and we knew something was wrong. He described Katie's bizarre and disruptive behaviors. It wasn't the typical screaming and crying … she'd slathered her menstrual blood on the bathroom walls. When they moved her to a single room, the staff found her naked on her bed, playing with her breasts, bra in her hand. Another time, she told a girl she was going to kill her because that girl angered her. The treatment team put her on suicide watch and was unsure if they could keep her.

We were in shock, having never even considered this school wasn't the right fit. We asked if it could just be a rocky first week. "It's doubtful," he said. He assured us they would help us locate a suitable treatment facility, and it sounded like they had already made up their minds. We hung up the phone in disbelief. We questioned why God allowed us to go through such turmoil, gave us a few days of rest, only to throw us back into the chaos.

Have I made a mistake or a terrible error in judgment? What have I missed in my extensive and analytical review? I felt I should have known or seen something I didn't. Paul assured me there was nothing I could have done differently, and we were both upset at Katie for making the situation worse. It was unbearable to fathom doing this again.

The previous summer, the four of us went to Europe for our family vacation. It was incredible to explore France, Austria, and Germany. Instead of using paper road maps, we relied on a global positioning system and trusted the voice that said, "Take the second exit toward Garmisch-Partenkirchen." While we never got lost, I didn't like not having a physical map showing we were headed the right way. This moment felt the same way … like we were operating without a map. We had to trust God was steering us in the right direction, which was difficult for my controlling personality.

When Paul and I were in Montana, I picked up a green bumper sticker that read, "Get Lost in Montana." It had served as a bookmark, but evoked mixed feelings because I hoped placing her at a residential treatment center was just a detour. But after the call from the case manager, it looked like the road ahead was longer and more uncertain than we hoped. We definitely felt lost.

A week later, we got a call at 6:45 a.m., asking for advice. Katie had been crying on the floor for an hour. I wanted to scream, *"You are the professionals. You figure it out."*

Instead, I said, "I don't know."

Later, Katie called to say how miserable she was.

"I cannot make it here much longer," she cried. "They aren't helping me."

My heart broke. With Katie's reactive attachment disorder and sensory integration issues, a hug wouldn't ease her pain. Nothing we did ever helped, other than letting time pass. But I also wondered if she thought Paul and I would swoop in and rescue her by being dramatic. At home, we didn't require her to do anything but take her medication because we were afraid of what she might do. But there, the staff were better equipped to handle mental health emergencies, and I was sure she didn't like that they pushed her. Paul and I were just grateful she was safe and, if we were brutally honest, that the problem wasn't right in front of us. The break from chaos and trauma was desperately needed.

One morning I read the book of Job in the Bible,

searching for comfort. Job was a blameless and upright man who feared God and shunned evil. Satan wanted to test Job and asked God for permission. God consented, and Job maintained his integrity throughout the trials. At one point, Job said, "Surely God, you have worn me out." The phrase ricocheted around in my head throughout the day.

God, I am indeed worn out. I know you can move mountains and calm the seas, so can you please just help us … please make some of our pieces fit together… even simple things like having people return my calls and paving the way for insurance claims.

Paul and I both believed God was allowing things to unfold as they should. But we couldn't understand why the path wasn't smoother. Job weathered the storm without turning his back on God, and in the end, God blessed him. We tried to keep that same faith and hoped God would provide for us, too.

Our small support group at church brought meals, sent cards, and offered notes of encouragement. One sweet woman even sent us a check for $350 to cover one day at this facility. Paul and I felt supported, but nothing relieved the increasing pressure of the unknown.

One month into her stay in Montana, the treatment facility unequivocally told us they couldn't keep Katie. We were still stuck and didn't know what to do. In searching for Katie's next home, I completed endless application packets, researched and analyzed data on treatment facilities, and took copious notes on my iPad. One place said she was too high-functioning, another too low. The insurance company liaison and I discussed placements, and she shot down my ideas because they weren't part of their network. In frustration, I suggested she research the seventy-five places I'd evaluated. She disagreed.

Finding an answer absorbed every waking moment, yet no one shared my urgency. The pace was unrelenting between working, serving on the elementary school board, and acting as Katie's case manager/advocate. My brain contemplated and rearranged hundreds of data points, disrupting my sleep and causing me to snap at people unnecessarily. The thought of making another mistake was paralyzing. No one was helping, so the solution rested on my shoulders. Paul focused on getting his mom situated in a nearby senior living community, working and drinking to relieve his stress. Nick had to fend for himself.

During those weeks, an encouraging devotional by Joel Osteen appeared in my inbox. It said,

> The same God that opens doors will close doors. Maybe you prayed and didn't get the job you wanted, or a relationship didn't work out. It's easy to allow rejection to lead to discouragement and think that God is not working in your life. But God sees the bigger picture for your life. He knows where every road is leading and where the dead ends are. Proverbs 20:24 says, 'A person's steps are directed by the Lord. How then can anyone understand their own way?' When you realize you are in the palm of God's hand and that

> nothing happens without His divine purpose, then you will begin to see and realize that the closed doors are just as important as the open doors.

I tried to trust God knew what he was doing.

One night, I threw out a new idea to Paul. "What do you think about a different approach to this situation? Katie has so many diagnoses, but we don't know if they are all still applicable. She's never received an autism diagnosis in all these years, but her case manager thinks she has it. What if we could get her into a facility for a comprehensive assessment in the short term? Then with that information, we could find the right longer-term placement?"

As he usually did, he concurred, respecting my logic and reasoning. Plus, he appreciated the homework I was doing. Looking back on my notes, I found a facility in Utah I'd spoken with two months earlier. I ruled them out because it wasn't a long-term placement. But they offered exactly what I described to Paul. The more I considered it, the more it made sense. The next day, I called to discuss their program again. It seemed to be the right fit, and I pleaded with the insurance company liaison to look at it. A few days later, she came around. I'm not sure if she was just tired of my relentless badgering or genuinely believed it was the right solution, but she recommended it to her bosses. Then she fought for coverage as an in-network provider, so our cost was a smaller portion of the $600-day price tag. After a few nail-biting days, the insurer and the facility agreed on a contract. What a miracle! How often does an insurance giant care about one individual? It was a huge win. I was grateful God had opened the right door for her and it felt like my persistence and tenacity finally paid off. The facility had a bed available for her, and we planned to move her to Utah the following week.

Chapter Five

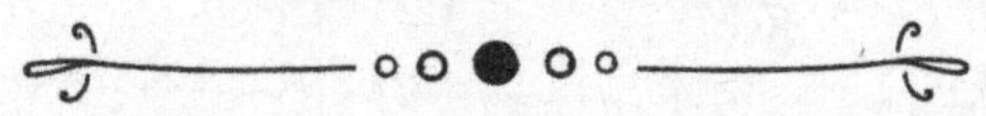

I am beginning to learn that it is the sweet, simple things of life which are the real ones after all.

Laura Ingalls Wilder

A segment about prayer came on the radio as I was doing errands before Paul and I returned to Montana to move Katie. The line that struck me was "God is not a vending machine"—a concept I still hadn't embraced. The last few months had been grueling, and the constant stress took its toll, causing sleepless nights and elevated blood sugars, detrimental to my diabetic body.

I believed God could resolve every issue we were facing, but He hadn't, and I questioned why. The notion that *only* bad Christians experienced hardship and *oly* well-behaving Christians were blessed played like a song stuck on repeat. *What had I done, or not done, to deserve this?*

As a child, everything went well for our family, and I attributed it to being upright, and maybe uptight, Christians. I'd grown up thinking if I were good, God would answer my prayers, as if choosing from a vending machine. But now, I learned that was untrue.

Childhood memories fluttered through my mind, like subdued photographs with a classic 70s vibe–the colors unsaturated and dulled with a yellow tinge. Those snapshots reflected our modest yet cheerful world. As a wholesome and respectable family of four, we loved God and each other, like relatives and generations before us—a lineage of decency, integrity, and goodness.

Our tri-level, olive-colored house in an Illinois suburb sat on a cul-de-sac in a newer neighborhood. We gathered in the orange plaid kitchen for dinner every night and spent most of our time watching *Little House on the Prairie* and Cubs' games or playing Uno in the red, white, and blue family room. From the backyard, the grade school peeked through a line of poplar trees. My younger brother, Brian, and I walked there with neighborhood kids but begged our mom to drive us the half-mile on snow days. On winter mornings, when the snowdrifts were deep, we sat by the large brown console in the living room, listening to the announcer reading a list of school closures. It took forever to get through the alphabet to the W's, but we cheered when he named our school. Wrapped in scarves, hats, and gloves, we'd hike to the small hill at the top of the street to sled into the berm the snowplow left in front of our driveway.

Most days, though, I preferred being alone in my apple green bedroom with cozy shag carpet. Dolls and stuffed animals lined up like students in a classroom, complete with coordinated bulletin boards and lesson plans. A stack of library books—everything from autobiographies to *Little House on the Prairie*, the *Hardy Boys, and* the *Choose Your Own Adventure* series—sat next to my bed to quench my voracious appetite for reading.

I was like a warm apple pie, subtly sweet and wholesome, intermingled with a hint of spices that oozed goodness. My feelings were visible on my chubby cheeks and sparkling hazel eyes.

Occasionally, the rotten apple emerged unintentionally when I was bored. One time, my buddy and I sat under an enormous oak tree picking dandelions and scouring the grounds for acorns, which we tossed at moving cars to pass the time. Our moms were coordinating yet another church project, and we were told to play nicely while we waited for them to finish. It was fun until an irate driver stopped and chewed us out for being naughty little children.

During the summer, the library reading contest screamed my name. Prizes, like faux-leather-bound anthologies and beautifully lettered certificates on parchment paper, were awarded to those who read the most books. So, I went each day and checked out the maximum number of books that would fit in my bike basket and backpack. My mom made me ride there because she knew my desire to read would override my general loathing of exercise. But the ten-minute ride, which felt like an hour, curled my dark bangs from the sweat on my forehead, and I hated how it looked. But when I arrived, sweet older ladies, who smelled like roses, read my book reports and praised my impeccable handwriting. Their attention and approval brought a blissful glow to my face, like sunshine reflecting off fresh snow.

For family vacations, we loaded up the station wagon we called the Jolly Green Giant with our tent trailer in tow and visited almost every state, from the Black Hills of South Dakota to Washington, D.C., and the Great Lakes. Park rangers captivated us with entertaining stories around campfires. S'mores filled our bellies while the fresh smell of the forest filled our lungs. In other places, swimming pools provided a welcome relief to long hours on the road. We gleefully sang songs, tuned in to radio dramas, played trivia games, and looked for license plates from across the country. Everything I ever wanted, except maybe more books, was right there next to me.

Our family was also very involved in church, where we showed up for some activity multiple days each week. Brian and I attended a youth group called AWANA (Approved Workman Are Not Ashamed) on Wednesday nights during the school year. We earned badges and pins for memorizing Bible verses and performing good works in our little red vests with grey trim. A favorite leader drew me in with her sparkling laugh. Her plump face and dark hair highlighted bright eyes that smiled when I recited my verses flawlessly. My face glowed with her praise and approval, and I wanted to be just like her.

Later that year, someone caught one of our church leaders embezzling money. My dad served on the leadership board, and I recall a heaviness as he, as part of that board, encouraged the embezzler to confess his sin. He refused. Months afterward, the embezzler had a heart attack and died while in his forties or fifties. This incident got filed away as a "don't screw up or God might kill you" scenario. It cemented the verse in Galatians that said, *"A man reaps what he sows. The one who sows to please his sinful nature, from that nature will reap destruction; the one who sows to please the Spirit, from the Spirit will reap eternal life."*

I adored my father, who was hardworking, honorable, and loving, even when he was busy with his demanding job at a college and volunteering at church. He took time to build me a white dollhouse with green trim that was very stylish with its pink shag carpet. Brian and I walked around the neighborhood gathering newspapers and cans to recycle, and I used my earnings to buy doll furniture and accessories. I created decor from scraps found around the house. Like a typical brother, Brian loved to annoy me by messing it up, and I would dramatically wail to my mom, "Brian is wrecking everything again!"

Each year, dad and I dressed up for a Christmas date. Dinner out was a special treat because it wasn't a prudent use of limited dollars. My dad disliked shopping, but this one time a year, he cheerfully picked out the perfect gifts for my mom and Brian. The time we spent hanging out in the garage listening to Dodger games on the radio while he worked on the cars and slaving over my math homework together made me feel special. My heart swelled when he presented me with a gold heart pendant, the note inside in his precise, architect-like handwriting, read, *"Above all else guard your heart, for it is the wellspring of life."* Proverbs 4:23

My mom seemed to be the perfect homemaker. When my dad returned from work each night, she had a nutritious dinner ready. No matter how many volunteer projects and chores she completed during the day, her hair and makeup were perfect. She excelled at everything and was such an extraordinary and productive volunteer that my dad stuck a note next to our wall-mounted phone that reminded her to "just say no."

One winter, we took a brief vacation to southern Illinois. It excited me to stay in a hotel with a pool instead of our well-worn tent trailer. While my parents unloaded the car, Brian and I checked out our room. Brian found some matches on the table and lit them. The room filled with smoke, and the fire alarm beeped loudly. Mom and the hotel staff rushed to our room. She was furious and embarrassed. I'd never seen her so angry. After everyone else left, she used terms I'd never heard before and that she hasn't used since. I didn't know what to do. My parents didn't get angry. I'd never heard them argue and rarely detected impatience in their tone. But after that night, I never wanted to draw the ire of her or anybody else. If I just adhered to the rules, I felt I would be appropriate and lovable.

When I was nine, our family flew to the west coast for Christmas to visit my relatives—my first time on a plane.

We stayed at my aunt and uncle's house in Oregon, and Christmas presents surrounded the beautiful tree. While Brian shot BB guns with our cousins, I surveyed the gifts. I discovered a package with my name and prayed it was the clogs I'd been coveting. I unwrapped it only to find a leather-working kit. My heart sank as my aunt appeared in the doorway with her apron, spatula in hand, with a disapproving look. As I re-wrapped the box, I tried to hold on to the tears of disappointment, devastated. Those clogs were my ticket to being more socially acceptable in the fashion department. My mom was an excellent seamstress. But the clothes she made weren't the Granimals, Jordache jeans, or Calvin Kleins the other kids wore. I was never cool, and without those clogs, I never would be.

It was hard to muster the energy to do much during that trip, and my mom thought I had a cold. But the sluggishness lingered for months. Not an hour would go by without me gulping from the bathroom faucet and then needing to use the toilet for the millionth time. My tongue felt like it was covered with paste. The only benefit was that I lost weight but didn't know if it was worth it because I felt awful all the time. My ten-year-old physical in June showed astronomically high urine sugar. The doctor admitted me to the hospital right away with the diagnosis of Juvenile, or Type 1, diabetes.

The diabetes educator warned us about the life-threatening nature of the disease and how crucial strict management of food and sugar levels was. Urine was collected in a cup twice a day and then I dipped a test strip into it. After a minute, the results appeared, and it told me about the general range of my sugar levels. A nurse taught me to give insulin shots on an orange and then my thigh, stomach, and arms. A thin dietician gave me a pamphlet that listed an apple, half of a banana, or ten grapes as one fruit on the diabetic meal exchange. She wrote a food plan describing what to eat each day—one protein, one starch, and one fat for breakfast. She wrote a similar prescription for lunch and dinner. It didn't matter if I was hungry or what I craved—I was simply to follow the plan. A good day was a day with no reactions—low blood sugar—and no high ones. Foods became "good" or "bad," which I equated to being a good or bad person. The lightness of childhood evaporated. The seriousness of the disease turned my desire to be good and do well into an evil inner critic, constantly evaluating and judging my performance. Naïve childhood beliefs still played out in my life, even in my forties, and I needed to figure out how to reconcile them while keeping my faith.

Chapter Six

Faith in God includes faith in His timing.

John Maxwell

Paul and I flew to Montana to move Katie to Utah. She was excited to see us and to leave the "mean girls" in her home. Her autistic-like characteristics and reactive attachment disorder, which prevented children from forming appropriate attachments, made it hard for her to navigate relationships, making any situation with other people challenging.

We tried to make the best of the nine-hour drive to Salt Lake City. She looked forward to playing her Nintendo DS and having quiet time without a bunch of teenagers around. Paul and I enjoyed the scenery and listening to our favorite music, but there was an underlying tension about the unknown looming ahead. Katie was quiet most of the time, but did share one revelation she had made over the past five and a half weeks—she was emotionally strong. She talked a lot about not getting help or having access to food every time she was hungry. During the weekend, she was delighted to have access to unlimited snacks and as much macaroni and cheese as she wanted.

Our route took us through Yellowstone National Park, Old Faithful, and the Grand Tetons. The incredible scenery was therapeutic for all of us. Our hotel in Jackson Hole had an impressive outdoor pool, which Katie liked so much she said she wanted to return for her sixteenth birthday. It was nice to hear her looking forward to something instead of constantly talking about death.

Salt Lake City was scorching hot, yet Katie still wore her uniform of black yoga pants and a green sweatshirt. As usual, the temperature didn't affect her, but I also wondered if she was covering evidence of self-harm. The baggy clothes were part of her armor, her way of hiding from the world while in plain view. Fluctuating temperatures had never bothered her, which was yet another mystery

We celebrated her fourteenth birthday at a nice Italian restaurant, and she opened a few gifts. It was hard to know what to buy a child who wore the same clothes repeatedly and was only interested in video games, something she didn't have access to in treatment. But she had always been content with very little.

Over the weekend, Katie didn't express any fear or hesitation and said she was thankful to move on. She referred to this as her "long business trip" with a beginning and an end, much like Paul's frequent work trips.

Once we arrived in Salt Lake City, Katie immediately took to the staff. Like a typical kid with reactive attachment disorder, she tried to make a good impression. Her ability to fake it had been a problem many times before because Katie appeared higher functioning than was sustainable. It reminded me of grade school when she held it together at school but had melted down at home. When asked to do anything she didn't want to, or her emotions rolled out of balance, she was a different person —like a rag doll on the floor or a screaming banshee.

The treatment center looked more like a sterile hospital than a school campus, and Katie's most significant concern was access to food. The staff assured her meals and snacks would always be available as needed. Her fixation on food continued to surprise me since we'd always had plenty, but it was more noticeable than ever before.

The team's approach was to adjust her medication and monitor her blood levels and behaviors right away. The doctors planned testing in neuropsychology, speech pathology, brain mapping, learning disabilities, non-verbal learning disorders, and academic testing, along with a comprehensive medical evaluation. Paul and I completed individual parent assessments as well. These were challenging because of Katie's extremes and my fear the evaluator would consider me a terrible parent. I always protected my perceived goodness.

Do you want me to answer on her hyper or depressed days? Should I reflect as the very best or worst version of myself? It could sound terrible or not as bad, depending on the day.

Katie's initial response was positive, the opposite of the previous residential treatment center, and it was much easier to leave her. We prayed we would get the needed information.

Just one week earlier, we were on vacation with Nick, watching him surf in Southern California, awaiting word from the insurance company and the facility about a possible placement agreement, and now she was there. This seemed to be the chaotic pace of our lives, with the situation changing daily. We had to be flexible about everything, something challenging for two ambitious, driven personalities.

Over those summer months, Nick had a lot of freedom as I focused on Katie's treatment. Paul and I felt terrible for him and almost always said yes to his requests. Once Katie moved out, it was much more comfortable for him to invite friends over, and we started seeing his buddies again. One weekend right before school started, he had two friends staying the night, and they played video games in the man cave, our converted garage. Paul fell asleep on our bed after drinking a martini or two, unbothered by the warm temperature.

When I tried to fall asleep later that evening, I tossed and turned. It was hot even though our ceiling fan was on full speed with our windows open, one of the few nights we needed air conditioning each year. The intermittent noise from the road behind us, a favorite place for motorcycles to speed, kept me awake.

Then I heard a strange sound, like a car braking and stopping, which was odd because there was no reason to stop behind our house. The bushes rustled, and it sounded like someone was in our backyard. I got up to look but couldn't see anything in the darkness. A knock at the door soon followed. Paul didn't move, so I threw on my clothes to answer it. A police officer asked for permission to go into my backyard and if I knew anything about lemons being thrown. I said I didn't, but there were three boys in my garage who might.

The police officer followed me into the garage. The lights were off, and the boys faked like they were asleep. But they soon came clean about tossing lemons from our tree over the fence. It turned out that they not only hit the front of a Honda Accord, but they'd also hit the police car that followed when the driver called the police.

As we stood outside on the driveway, waiting for the other boys' parents to pick them up, the driver laid into the boys. She said they caused extensive damage to her old car, not only with the lemons but with the sandy towels they grabbed to clean off the hood afterward. The police officer negotiated a compromise where the boys would pay for the damage, and the driver wouldn't file charges. Since it had happened at my house, I took responsibility for dealing with her. Nick and his friends weren't malicious, they were just bored, and we'd had a tough summer. Paul slept through the whole incident, which reminded me of just how alone I was.

Katie should have been starting high school at the end of August, but instead, she was in Utah. The first week at the new facility went better than her first week at the other one, and we didn't get any calls from the staff. Her first call home revolved around the fact she could eat as much as she wanted. She seemed content, but Paul and I anxiously awaited the report and direction on what to do next.

Within a week, however, negative behaviors started again, hindering staff from completing their assessments. Katie was mean and aggressive with the other kids, and they refused to be around her. She didn't understand what she was doing wrong. Katie had never been successful in peer relationships because she couldn't read emotions and didn't understand sarcasm. But, once again, she was bringing it upon herself. I wrestled with my frustration that she was being herself. While I believed people should be authentic, the real Katie was hard to deal with.

As a child, I could have never gotten away with behavior like hers. My parents would have disciplined me for misbehaving as she did. No consequence motivated Katie to change her behavior, though. In fact, I did not know what motivated Katie at all, other than pushing me away. I constantly asked if she had control over her behavior and was manipulating me or genuinely powerless.

By the end of five weeks, the facility was ready to provide their analysis of Katie, and a neuropsychologist, psychiatrist, and therapist summarized their findings during an intense ninety-minute call. That Katie had a multitude of issues was no surprise. In some ways, it was a relief to see it on paper because it explained why it was so difficult to manage since the treatments and therapies often conflicted.

The doctors concluded Katie was on the autism spectrum but attributed her autistic-like characteristics to the reactive attachment disorder. Her primary diagnosis was reactive attachment disorder followed by a cornucopia of others including ADHD, pervasive developmental disorder, oppositional defiance disorder, major depressive disorder, anxiety, fetal alcohol exposure, speech and language impairments, a math learning disability, trichotillomania, and sensory integration issues. The team recommended that Katie go to long-term placement for at least eighteen months, focusing on the reactive attachment disorder. I could not imagine Katie being away for another year and a half, but was not ready to have her home, either. It had been three months, and while our home was more peaceful, having her away felt odd. She was still in our daily lives as we braced for crisis calls from her facility.

Paul still traveled a lot for work, and we were disconnected, sharing functional details but not much emotional support. He worked. I worked. We kept Nick and our dog, Charlie, alive. But we weren't living. We were existing. Barely.

Chapter Seven

Once you hear the details of victory,
it is hard to distinguish it from a defeat.

Jean-Paul Sartre

The team treatment call, with the recommendation to find a long-term program to help Katie build appropriate attachments, weighed heavily on me. Like it or not, it was up to me to again fit all the pieces together. No one else was going to decide where she should go or even make a strong recommendation.

After more late-night research, a facility in Missouri, specializing in reactive attachment disorder, appeared as one of the few programs in the country with this primary focus. The admissions counselor and I discussed Katie's diagnoses and history. They conferred with her existing facility and then informed us Katie would be a good fit for their program. They even offered us a partial scholarship

—and enormous relief since we continued to be unsure how to manage the financial aspect of her treatment.

Meanwhile, we met with her school district again, and they miraculously agreed that residential placement was the only appropriate option for her. But the schools they offered were not equipped to meet her needs. They only knew Katie on paper and didn't understand the nuances of her diagnoses. The district wouldn't place her at the school I found because it wasn't on the California Department of Education's (CDE) approved school list. After reviewing why the list of one hundred approved schools wasn't appropriate for Katie's unique needs, I worked with the new facility to get it approved. After the school submitted their paperwork to the state, I badgered the CDE staffer, just as with our insurance company, so she couldn't say no.

Katie needed to leave Utah because the funding agreement had expired. Paul and I made arrangements to move her and hoped the district would come around. Paul and I flew to Salt Lake City to pick Katie up and she looked healthier, with eleven additional pounds on her thin frame. Her eyes were brighter, and her acne wasn't as inflamed. She had showered and even had on clean clothes. The three of us flew to Kansas City and then drove several hours on two-lane roads through farmland to southern Missouri. Katie was vibrating with anticipation. She tugged on her hair, and the bald patch confirmed her anxiety. Meeting new girls and understanding the group's social order terrified Katie. I reminded her she would only be the new girl once at this school. But this felt hollow since she'd been the new girl three times already this year.

The facilities were impressive, with their new school building and indoor dog training space. It thrilled Katie to meet the new litter of golden retrievers that she'd work with as part of the attachment program. There was nothing better than puppy snuggles for dog lovers like Katie.

The school sat on a magnificent, enormous lake. The gentle lapping of water against the shore and expansive oak trees provided a sense of calm. I wanted to feel optimistic, but given our earlier experience, it was hard to trust my feelings. As we walked around the campus, I felt responsible for Katie's mental health and wished we had known enough to see the warning signs indicating she was as emotionally unstable as she was. The adoption agency and the medical professionals should have educated us better on reactive attachment disorder and its consequences. I wished I'd done more to understand it in the early days, when hints of it came up. But professionals in our area didn't know much about it and it just fell off my list with everything else there was to learn about parenting Katie. Somehow, I still believed if I had more information, the outcome would have been different.

After meeting her team and seeing where she'd spend her time, Paul and I returned home. The travel and emotions took their toll as we sat in the airport, eyes glazed over. We were veterans in a battle we never intended to wage, fighting for our daughter's health and wellness. We never wanted to join this exclusive club. And though we should have felt some sort of optimism, by this point, we held everything loosely because we'd been disappointed so many times before. It was Katie's third placement in five months.

Working with the district was agonizingly slow. Their goal puzzled me. I didn't understand why they continued to make everything so arduous. As we arrived at yet another meeting, I tried to keep a lid on my exasperation. I prayed God would literally hold my tongue if I were about to say something I shouldn't. I had had enough.

Thankfully, I didn't lose my temper, and Paul shared this email with our friends and family afterward.

> I wanted to give an update on our meeting this morning. Valerie should really be the one to provide the update, but she is swamped. On the plus side of this coming from me, she would never say about herself what an awesome, relentless, intelligent, articulate advocate she is for Katie! Our meeting lasted three hours. There were varying points of tension, but, overall, we left amicably and with a potential settlement agreement for Katie's placement and their funding of it. The district needs to run it by their lawyers once more, but we expect to have it back this week.

My perseverance and tenacity paid off when the Department of Education approved this new facility as a certified non-public school. This decision was critical, not just for Katie, but for all children in California with RAD. Research shows that between fifty and eighty percent of adopted children have attachment disorder symptoms because of early maltreatment, neglect, and abuse. Having this resource would help Katie and so many others. For us, approval meant the district could place her there and pay for it, which was a tremendous relief. However, though we won this particular battle, we felt bloodied and bruised.

A few weeks later, Paul and I met up with college friends at our college reunion. It was great to connect and hear their positive updates, but harder to share our struggles. When we were students, it felt like the campus only had shiny, happy, perfect people. No one seemed to struggle. But now, as an adult, I discarded the notion of perfection —with nothing to lose by being honest. Some of our friends had read our blog posts and shared how our journey had impacted them. I walked away from that weekend, believing if the road was going to be difficult either way, I might as well learn from it and help someone else by sharing my experience.

It was so different from my high school and college years when I held everything close to my heart. After high school, I chose Westmont College, where I could attend tuition-free since my dad worked there. Westmont provided exceptional education and a summer camp-like setting with incredible professors, staff, and students. Life-long friendships developed.

My sophomore year, the opportunity to go to an off-campus program presented itself, and I spent the fall semester at Hawaii Loa College on Oahu. It was easy ... far easier academically than Westmont. Being away from home and not being Ron or Jan's daughter or Brian's sister was refreshing. I was just Valerie, the girl from California with dark, curly hair.

Unlike at Westmont, where there were four girls to every boy, Hawaii Loa had a more balanced population, and boys started paying attention to me. Basketball players stopped by my room and asked to hang out. My favorite was a tall, dark-skinned forward from London who recited poetry outside my window and was intrigued by me as a California girl.

After my carefree semester in Hawaii, I moved to Washington, D.C. for the spring semester at American University, which was better aligned with my ambition and drive. My program concentrated on a unique aspect of journalism each week, exposing us to various career opportunities. The class met with the White House Press Secretary, discussed network broadcasting with David Brinkley at NBC, and visited the Supreme Court. Everything about the program and the city inspired me, and I was optimistic about my future and the possibility of a fulfilling career.

My two roommates drank beer every weekend and acted kooky when they did. They weren't out of control. They just acted dumb and laughed at stupid situations. I didn't see the appeal of it. Then one of my friends persuaded me to go barhopping with her in Georgetown and got me a fake ID. It was uncharacteristic of me, the rule follower, to do something so outrageous. I enjoyed my Diet Coke, convinced I'd be caught with my fake ID. The following Monday, it felt good to have something to contribute when my classmates and I talked about the previous weekend.

Part of the journalism program included an internship, and the Cherry Blossom Parade hired me as their coordinator. The parade is a massive annual event celebrating the gift of cherry blossoms from Japan. It raises money for the Downtown Jaycees to help needy kids. Each week, I reviewed applications for bands wanting to participate, wrote press releases, and contacted major corporations asking for sponsorships.

On parade day, a group of Marines helped and then came to the volunteer after-party. The parade had gone off with no problems, and I felt relieved and relaxed. Most of the volunteers were older businesspeople. But the Marines were my age, entertaining and flirtatious as they sipped their cold beers. One kept talking to me, and I felt giddy with the attention. I realized I liked the effect alcohol had on them because I became more attractive. I was cute and witty and fun to be with, things I didn't think about myself, and it was emotionally intoxicating.

When I returned to Westmont for my junior year, I devoted every waking moment to managing *The Horizon,* our student newspaper. Our team crammed into the small office with its stale coffee aroma. Depeche Mode pulsed through the speakers as we wrote, edited, and argued about grammar in the weekly paper. The job's fast pace, intensity, and responsibility activated me like the final display in a fireworks show, and I barely remember anything else that year.

As the semester ended, I worked out a less strenuous schedule for my senior year—a much-needed break before I graduated and launched my yet-to-be-determined impactful career. I rented a room off-campus, registered for enrichment classes, and secured an internship with a political consulting and communications firm.

One of my summer tasks included a routine visit to my doctor. Afterward, he ordered a slew of tests, including a 24-hour urine test, which was new to me. When he didn't like the results, he had me repeat it several times. Then he referred me to a nephrologist who presented a crushing diagnosis—diabetic kidney disease, which would lead to kidney failure and death without a transplant. The nephrologist ordered a kidney biopsy to evaluate the damage. As I laid on my abdomen, the surgeon instructed me to hold my breath as he stuck a long needle in my back. With no anesthesia, I felt every centimeter as it went into my kidney. Tears leaked from my eyes as I held my breath and tried not to cry out from the pain.

My parents requested a second opinion from a friend and UCLA physician who assessed the tissue samples and confirmed the diagnosis. The damage was irreversible. My doctors would monitor my kidney function until it got so low that a transplant was necessary to stay alive.

The film *Steel Magnolias* came out that summer. Julia Roberts played a diabetic mother with kidney disease who died when her child was young. I sobbed in the theater, convinced that this was going to be my story. Pregnancy could never be part of my future, and I was distressed at the thought of not having a family.

At twenty-one years old, I assumed I had my entire life ahead of me. But now it appeared I didn't. I guessed I had five years before a transplant was inevitable and grappled with serious questions. My big dream was to work for *Newsweek* and fall in love with a fantastic guy, but I didn't think any of that could happen now.

What have I always dreamed of doing? If I only have five years, what do I want to do? How can I make a meaningful impact on the world? Will anyone remember me for anything special after I die? Will anyone love me and my broken body?

The diagnosis was cruel because I'd always been so good and followed the rules. I didn't drink any alcohol until after I was twenty-one. I never smoked, didn't do drugs. If I had just been good in one more area—my diabetes management—I wouldn't be in this situation. In my rebelliousness with my disease, I'd only hurt myself. School felt pointless

While the kidney disease didn't cause pain, it wreaked havoc on my emotions. The messages swirling around in my head made me want to die. As a kid, I heard I was overly sensitive and learned to suppress my feelings to be a resilient, productive problem-solver. My friends always turned to me for support. Now, I had to rely on them. It was challenging to disclose my situation, even to the handful of people closest to me.

My diabetes control took priority over everything. I followed a strict diet, exercised faithfully, and went to the acupuncture appointments my mom arranged. My professors understood when I explained my health had taken priority over school. A college degree felt less important than living for long as I could.

Chapter Eight

Occasionally, weep deeply over the life you hoped for.
Grieve the losses. Feel the pain.
Then wash your face. Trust God.
And embrace the life you have.

John Piper

Despite the favorable decision from the school district about funding Katie's placement in Missouri, that fall was hard for many reasons. Katie had been in treatment for four months when the doctor diagnosed my eight-year-old nephew with leukemia, and my mom found out she had kidney cancer. It felt like a pile of snow had been dumped on us, and we didn't have a shovel. *How could God allow this to happen to our family? Didn't we have enough already?*

Well-meaning people often said, "God has a wonderful plan for your life" or "God will only give you what you can handle." But when your head is hovering below the water's surface, these phrases aren't comforting. Yet, I had said those exact things in the years before struggles plagued our family, or at least when I pretended it wasn't as bad as it was. Ultimately, I decided God gave us what He wanted to handle through us, and our job was to rely on Him.

In that year of darkness, throwing myself into work and projects helped me maintain my sanity. It was easier to organize knife drawers and design beautiful documents than to sit in the uncertainty of our lives. While we didn't need to be vigilant about whether Katie was self-harming that day or put up with her moods, our stress levels remained high as we waited for some other tornado to come at us. My office was my refuge and my computer my best friend, as I continued searching for anything else that could help Katie. While I wasn't the sweet, patient, affectionate mother I thought Katie needed, I could advocate for her. It relieved my feelings of being an incompetent mother.

With the larger tasks completed, I resorted to smaller ones, like cleaning out files and closets that didn't need tidying. With my magic eraser in hand, I scanned the walls for any mark that needed cleaning or a paint touch-up. It was so symbolic of my life. The exterior could appear pristine while the interior was crumbling.

Paul's response to the stress was working and drinking and then drinking more. Like me, he craved the ability to control everything and, when he couldn't, he numbed himself with martinis and fell asleep on the couch. Most Friday nights, Paul went to happy hour with his co-workers. He invited me, but I usually declined. The drinking environment was unappealing, but there were other factors to consider. *Should I go so I could make sure Paul got home safely? Or should I stay home instead, hoping he wouldn't overindulge because he had to drive?*

On one of those nights, he came home late as I was reading in bed. He mumbled hello and started taking off his clothes. His toe caught on his pants, and he fell, kicking our mirrored closet doors instead, shattering the glass. He startled and then fell into bed. I froze. *How could you break a mirrored door and then fall into bed? What about the glass on the floor? Did he expect me to clean it up?*

Instead of forcing the issue, I did what was so typical of me, handling anything that went wrong to avoid conflict. While Paul was the fixer at work, I had become the fixer at home. But had I also become an enabler?

The next day, he left for work before I got up, and I didn't know if he realized what had happened the previous evening. Ordinarily, I would have asked my dad for help but was too embarrassed to say Paul had been drunk again and broken the door. So, I called a handyman to take care of it.

When I met Paul my senior year of college, I didn't picture this for our life. We met at a Phi Kappa Phi lecture I was covering for the newspaper, and he was smart enough to be in the academic society. The girl between us took copious notes, and we both asked her to share them, then debated who should get them first. My newspaper deadline preempted the class assignment he had, so I won and promised to deliver them to him afterward. It wasn't love at first sight, but there was interest on both sides, and we started dating a few weeks later.

Paul's sarcasm, intelligence, and wit made him attractive. A talented pianist, he was just my type—tall, dark, and handsome … wealthy, and well-dressed. He appreciated my spunky yet helpful personality and showed it with flowers and love notes.

Mutual friends said we'd either fall in love and get married, or we'd kill each other as competitive, achievement-oriented individuals. We fell in love quickly. Within two months of dating, we were talking about marriage.

He wasn't an average Westmont guy, and I liked that. It seemed Westmont men preferred women whose career goals were to stay at home, raise babies, and excel in the PTA. And that wasn't me. My dreams and plans for an extraordinary life did not intimidate Paul.

Something was exciting about the fact that he wasn't a cookie-cutter version of me. His bad boy side intrigued me. He'd partied in high school but landed at Westmont with academic scholarships, defying my impression of partiers as losers. On the other end, my parents always knew where I was, what I was doing, and who my friends were—and they had no reason not to trust me.

Paul also grew up in a Christian home. He was an only child, adopted at birth by his Russian parents. His dad was an abusive alcoholic, and Paul assured me he would never turn into his dad. Paul hated what his dad had done to him and his mom.

When we were dating, Paul's drinking never seemed excessive, except the time he blacked out at our friends' engagement party. He assured me it would never happen again, and I trusted him with little knowledge about alcoholism. I believed Paul would be a righteous man who never drank too much, and we'd have a perfect Christian family.

Paul checked all my boxes. Our shared vision for respectable jobs, volunteering at church, having children, material success, and living in a comfortable home in Santa Barbara made us a good match. I believed our future family would adhere to script I had seen played out in my childhood.

One night while watching a sitcom on television, the lead couple was rudely fighting, and I said, "No one acts that way."

Paul said, "Every family in America acts that way except for yours."

Despite our familial differences, Paul proposed on the first day of spring after asking my dad for my hand in marriage. We'd dated for two years, and it seemed like the right time. With my event management experience, wedding planning was exciting. My parents gave us a lump sum of money and said that anything above that would come from our pockets and anything we didn't spend would be ours to keep. It disappointed me I wasn't able to include my mom more in the planning. We weren't that close, but I thought this traditional mother-daughter experience might bridge the distance between us. However, Paul wanted to provide input on everything from the colors and flowers to the bridesmaids' dresses, the music, and the food. It felt like too much energy to merge my opinions with Paul's and my mom's, so I didn't include her in most decisions. They didn't necessarily clash. It just wasn't smooth.

During our pre-marital counseling with a couple from church, we talked about our families of origin and our experiences growing up. While he didn't have my idyllic childhood, we believed no problem or challenge was insurmountable and looked forward to marriage.

Six months later, we wed in a picture-perfect ceremony in the lovely Santa Barbara church we attended. During our reception, a string quartet played while we ate along with our two hundred guests. A picture of us, beaming in the back of a 1931 Model A Ford, even appeared in a glossy coffee-table book on wedding celebrations. It seemed perfect. We were young, happy, and in love with all the promise of a glorious future.

The next day, we left for a romantic honeymoon in Kauai. I looked forward to intimate moments with my husband. At twenty-four years old, I'd waited a long time, and although Paul had been intimate with previous girlfriends,

I expected he looked forward to this blessing of marriage with me. But he was more interested in playing the grand piano at the condominium we rented and enjoying cocktails and fancy food.

Before we got married, we visited a world-renown diabetes specialist to discuss birth control options. With my diabetic kidney disease, pregnancy could be life-threatening. The physician ordered various tests, including that same awful 24-hour urine collection I'd repeated over the years. Miraculously, the test showed my kidneys functioning at one hundred percent. The result was inconsistent with the previous biopsy, so the doctor had me repeat the test. When the results came back, it showed my kidneys were performing at one hundred percent, up from thirty percent during college.

What?!? Kidneys cannot regenerate, and yet mine were working as they should. While I had depended on God all my life, this was the first time I had experienced a miracle. It felt like a confirmation God rewarded those who followed Him. Paul and I were ecstatic, but I didn't know how to process the information and whether I could trust it. Paul and I shared this life-changing news with our families and a few close friends but didn't give it the emotional attention and significance it merited. It wasn't until years later I acknowledged what a miracle and gift it was.

When I turned twenty-six, we agreed we were ready to have a baby. We had purchased our first home, and both had stable, well-paying jobs. It seemed like the right time.

But then, two early miscarriages within nine months brought the dream of parenting to a startling halt. It was even more painful because two of our closest friends were pregnant, and it was tough to watch their growing bellies. After the miracle with my kidneys, I assumed pregnancy would be easy because I thought I deserved it. But after the second pregnancy, I knew I only had one more pregnancy in me and shared that with Paul. He understood. When I got pregnant again, we had a hard time getting excited. The nausea was awful. The sight of raw chicken or the smell of pesto, and the aroma of the Chinese food restaurant across from my office made me heave. But when those first twelve weeks passed, and I was still pregnant, we were overjoyed.

Meanwhile, Paul's parents were struggling financially and decided to move into the 900 square foot cabin his dad built for his babushka, who had passed. We went to Big Bear to help them pack and move, a dreadful experience. While packing and organizing were my forte, being amid the tension between Paul and his dad was uncomfortable. They'd never gotten along, and both had hot tempers—a bad combination for those around them. Paul was a mama's boy who could do no wrong. During his childhood, she treated him like a friend rather than a son. He was her ally in their family's struggle with the disease of alcoholism. It wasn't until years later when I went through a very similar situation with Paul's own battle with alcohol that I understood the complexity of his mom's impossible choices.

During one of those trips, Paul's mom and their pastor planned an intervention. My father-in-law had gotten two DUIs and was spiraling out of control. While they all met at church, I sat at their home, rubbing my sizable belly, and praying for a productive outcome. When Paul and his mom returned, they reported his dad stormed out of the church with a loaded gun in the backseat of his truck. We imagined the worst. I hoped that if he hurt anyone, it would only be himself. After an intense few days, he returned home, and I wasn't sure if I was relieved or disappointed. He wasn't a good man, nothing like my father.

The tension affected my body and the baby, and my doctor placed me on bed rest for the last two months of the pregnancy. He encouraged me to take it easy, which was a challenge as the holidays approached and the excitement of mommy-to-be nesting mode. I couldn't wait to hold the child I'd struggled to have.

Three weeks before my due date, the doctor induced me, common for diabetic mothers, and after forty hours of labor, they took the baby by c-section. Nicholas was born on January 8th at nine pounds, two ounces, and twenty inches long, with a full head of dark hair and crystal blue eyes. He was the perfect reward for a difficult pregnancy.

Being a mom was more wonderful than I'd ever envisioned. We read endless books, went to mommy/baby classes, and sang songs. Three mornings a week, he came to work with me, and my mom or Paul watched him on those afternoons. We explored parks, visited construction sites to watch trucks and heavy equipment, and played with finger paints on my days off. Life was whole with everything I ever desired—a husband, a son, a comfortable house, and a meaningful job. What more could I want?

Chapter Nine

Hardships often prepare ordinary people for an extraordinary destiny.

Voyage of the Dawn Treader

At the beginning of November, I soaked in the fall colors while visiting Katie at the facility in Missouri. On the positive side, Katie connected with her therapist and hadn't exhibited the behaviors she had in the other two places. But she claimed to be homesick and just wanted to check the boxes as quickly as she could to return to California. It was interesting because she was lonely at home, too, so I thought she just missed being alone in her room.

The school planned fun and therapeutic activities, but Katie was reluctant to admit any of them were enjoyable. Katie said the girls on her team were mean, and that bothered me. She described their rude remarks, and I shared my bullying experience.

"You were bullied? Why?" she asked.

I shared the story. "When I was in fifth grade, my class took a field trip to Chicago, which was an hour away from my school. After we went through the museum and got on the bus to return to school, I realized I needed to use the bathroom."

She stared at me with intense, emotionless eyes.

"Do you remember how bumpy those bus rides are?" I asked.

Katie didn't respond but continued to listen intently.

"Well, it made me have to use the bathroom even more. So, I thought about my options. If I told the teacher, she could ask the driver to stop, or I could pee my pants, or I could try to hold it."

She continued to stare at me.

"I knew I couldn't make it all the way home, so I told a chaperone. She told the teacher, who told the bus driver, who radioed the other bus driver. They had to find a bathroom for me in downtown Chicago. That's like one thousand times harder than finding a parking space at home."

Drool gathered on her chin. She was oblivious to it, attentive to my words.

"So, I got off the bus with the chaperone and went into the hotel bathroom. But everyone and I mean everyone, almost one hundred kids, knew I was the reason for the stop. They were all laughing when I got back on the bus.

Then they did it the next day at school, and even the next year."

"I didn't know you got bullied," she said flatly. It was as if she filed it somewhere in the recesses of her brain, never to be accessed again.

"It's really hard, but you can get through it like I did," I said.

What I didn't share was that it got worse after the diabetes diagnosis. Not only was I the potty problem girl, but I was also the chubby diabetic fighting additional pounds as my diabetes control improved. One girl threw crumpled paper wads at me and said nasty things to her seatmate. She demanded we fight. Thankfully, my mom pulled me from school before that happened, and the end of my sixth-grade year fizzled out.

So, I understood some of what Katie was going through. I tried to imagine how disturbing it must be for a girl who never understood the world and couldn't interpret a social dynamic. While the other girls were troubled, they didn't have autistic-like characteristics on top of the reactive attachment disorder. On the one hand, the girls' behavior angered me. On the other, I was upset Katie didn't even try.

Katie stayed on the fringes, away from their drama, by drawing and writing. She didn't have many hobbies beyond video games and being fixated on dogs and pillows, and generally lacked interest in others, so she didn't have friends.

After the long weekend with her, I drove the hour and a half back to the airport to catch my three flights home. While waiting in the airport, I thought about the months ahead. Typically, my Christmas cards would have been designed, ordered, and addressed before Thanksgiving. Most gifts would have been purchased, and I would be planning my holiday decorating and baking while listening to nonstop Christmas music. But this year, the season didn't have the same magic. With Katie in Missouri and the uncertainty of my family members' health, I had to really search for Christmas joy.

One of our family traditions was pizza with raw vegetables and ranch dip while decorating the tree. Even without Katie, I thought it might be a fun activity for Paul, Nick, Nick's girlfriend, and me. We picked out a seven-foot tree from the local hardware store, and Paul secured it on a stand in the living room. As I added the lights, he went upstairs. Nick and his girlfriend came in, and I asked what type of pizza they wanted. I went upstairs to check on Paul and found him sprawled across our bed, drunk. Couldn't he give me one evening of normalcy? I shut the door quietly and went back downstairs.

Nick asked, "Where's Dad? I'm hungry."

I said, "He's not feeling well. I'll order the pizza now."

Nick said, "Okay," and the three of us started hanging ornaments. Afterward, they left to be with their friends. The house was dark except for the lights on the tree and the glow of the fireplace. Tears streamed down my face, and all the feelings I didn't want to have crushed me.

The day after Christmas, Paul, Nick, and I flew to Missouri to visit Katie. The kids hadn't seen each other since June. Katie said Nick looked like a man, tall and broad-shouldered. She looked healthy, with more steady emotions. But the visit was awkward, with little to do. We weren't a board game or movie family. In the past, the best times had been at theme parks or sightseeing, and there were no sights to see in the middle of nowhere in the winter.

It was so different from when they were little. Nick was an exuberant big brother, sharing his colorful and exciting world. He showed Katie new and exciting things, and she was content to follow along. His constant stream of ideas entertained her. Nick biked and skated, designed obstacle courses for our dog, built forts, sang songs, and made life enjoyable. She observed him but couldn't engage fully in his world. Now they were in two completely different worlds without something to bridge the gap. We made it through the trip but were happy to return home.

Chapter Ten

We do not need to know the beginning of a child's story to change the ending

Fi Newood

While the challenges had not resolved and most likely wouldn't in the next twelve months, I hoped for peace and stability in the new year. We pressed on, knowing we could persevere. We'd done it through Katie's adoption process.

When Nicholas was a year old, Paul and I began investigating international adoption. Adoption had always been a consideration because of my kidneys and the fact Paul was adopted. So, deciding was easy. Because of Paul's heritage, we signed up with an agency placing children from the far east region of Russia. We both had dark brown hair, hazel eyes, and fair skin, and we thought our adopted child might look like us. Fifteen months later, they called to say they had a referral and faxed us the details. Our eyes scanned the form. *Mother smoked, used narcotics, and consumed alcohol ... mother had chronic lung issues ... multiple pregnancies and wasn't getting prenatal care ... fetus had delayed intrauterine development ... six on the Apgar scale at birth ... light case of perinatal encephalopathy of the post-hypoxia genesis ...*

We compared notes with the small group of parents using the same agency. Their referral documents had similar statements, and our agency said it was typical to have very little information. Most had references to development delays, but our coordinator assured us the kids they had placed were thriving. We consulted with our pediatrician and asked her to explain the medical report. She did and then requested we bring a video back for her review.

Despite her very rough beginning, we felt love, stability, attention, and medical treatment could improve this child's life. Of course, we also believed this was part of God's plan for our family. After a lot of prayer and discussion, we collected the paperwork and booked our flights to Vladivostok, Russia, to meet our daughter.

Several weeks and 7,000 miles later, we met our driver and our translator. They took us to Baby Home #2, an old, worn building on the outskirts of town. The colors of the paintings on the walls reminded me of the colorful nesting dolls Paul's parents displayed in his childhood home. The inside reeked of cabbage, and I tried not to breathe too deeply. The children were napping, and a staff member told us we'd have to come back the following day. My shoulders slumped. Didn't they know how far we'd traveled to meet this child?

The next afternoon, we returned to meet Lyubov, who we named Catherine and called Katie. Her enormous brown eyes and extraordinarily long eyelashes were stunning. She was tiny, the size of a six-month-old baby, even though she was nearly fifteen months old, and couldn't put weight on her legs. She barely moved around her six-foot-by-six-foot wooden playpen and made no sounds.

Katie was unsure about us as we tried to engage her with a few toys. She liked a soft photo cube with a picture of Nicholas and hesitantly touched Paul's glasses. The orphanage doctor described Katie's history and birth mother. Like many Russian women, she could not care for the baby and relinquished her parental rights at birth. We filed our intent to adopt with the court and returned to the orphanage.

Katie cried during most of the second visit. They offered us a bottle to feed her. She was ravenous and tried to suck the liquid down, but most of it dribbled down her chin. Her mouth couldn't form a seal around the nipple. I fed her soft food from a large serving spoon, but her little mouth and tongue couldn't reach the food. It was no surprise she was underweight—she couldn't eat enough.

Paul and I didn't feel an instant connection with Katie but wrote it off to being exhausted from the travel and stress of the adoption process. She seemed to have no interest in us either and we figured it was because we smelled and talked differently than her caregivers. Even without an immediate bond, we moved forward. We believed God would not allow us to make a mistake or give us more than we could handle. And we were sure our love for this tiny girl would grow. Surely she would flourish in a loving environment with access to food and medical care and grow up to be a healthy girl. Our family would be complete.

Just three weeks later, on December 10th, we flew back to Vladivostok to go to court and bring Katie home. One of the most vivid memories of the trip was having two documents notarized with our adoption coordinator and translator. We went to a massive building, thick with grit, in the middle of town. The notary was unwilling to authenticate our pediatrician's letter but agreed to sign some kind of statement. Her assistant, an older woman with decaying teeth, typed excruciatingly slow. I wanted to step in and do it myself! When she finally finished, she handed it to the translator, who sewed the two pages together and glued another small paper over the loose ends. The notary stamped the package, and the adoption coordinator delivered it to the judge. Later that afternoon, we got word our court date was the next day.

The judge was intimidating, with her blond bob and stern, makeup-free face, as she oversaw the proceedings. A state-appointed doctor made a case for urgent medical care. The judge nodded and then asked me several questions: How did Nicholas feel about the adoption? Who would help me take care of the children? How would our pediatrician provide treatment given the baby's significant medical needs? She then interviewed the education department representative and the prosecutor, then asked us to move into the hallway while she considered her decision.

Two or three minutes later, she called us back in. She smiled warmly and told us she had approved our adoption petition and waived the ten-day waiting period so we could be home with Nicholas for Christmas. We were ecstatic and relieved that our twenty-month journey was ending. We took a photo with her and then headed to the airline office to get on the waiting list for one of two weekly flights, hoping to make it home by Christmas.

The adoption agency staff took us to retrieve Katie and begin our journey as a family. We gave the orphanage a fax machine as a "gift" and hundreds of dollars' worth of baby clothing and food. It was customary for adoptive families to "contribute" to the orphanage, but I wondered how much supported the children rather than the orphanage director.

The first night in our hotel, Katie slept soundly on the red wool blanket given to us by the orphanage. It was good to have something that smelled and felt familiar. Over those next days, we got to know her while waiting for the adoption coordinator to return from Moscow with Katie's visa and passport.

Even though I had been a parent before, Katie's fragility terrified me. She was only fifteen pounds at sixteen months. In comparison, Nicholas was fifteen pounds at three months, and unlike him, she did everything slowly and tentatively. When I showered her in the hotel bathroom that sported jade green tiles, I feared my soapy hands would lose my grip on her. Every bone in her back was visible, and she screamed as water sprayed her body. It sounded like I was torturing her.

It was a blessing she couldn't crawl fast or far as we spent hours in that tiny hotel room. She sat on her red blanket and sucked her fingers, eyes wide with wonder, curiosity, and fear. She enjoyed picking up the cheerios we put on her blanket as we cautiously observed each other.

We watched endless table tennis and rugby matches so she could hear Russian, and we could pass the time. But some days, being cooped up in that room, with four inches of ice on the inside of the window, was too much. We placed her in a carrier strapped to my front like a kangaroo pouch and ventured out into the frigid air. It was bleak at twenty-seven degrees below zero with the windchill factor and reminded me of childhood winters in Illinois.

Paul read and spoke enough Russian to order food at restaurants and do essential shopping as armed security guards followed us around the market. It was amusing they thought we would steal something when our pocket change was probably more than what most of Vladivostok's residents made in a month.

Eight days after court, Katie's papers arrived, and we confirmed our flights from Vladivostok to Seoul to Los Angeles for the next day. Fifteen hours later, we arrived in California on December 23rd. The sight of my mom and dad, Paul's parents, and Nicholas brought streams of tears to my eyes. I was so grateful to be home. When the kids met for the first time, Katie cried, and Nicholas wanted to play. He was thrilled to meet his sister.

The next evening, we went to the Christmas Eve service at church and were asked to do the advent reading and candle lighting. It felt unreal to stand before our church family, many of whom had prayed for us for more than a year, with our two children. It felt like the most challenging part was over. We couldn't wait to start our journey as a family of four.

The first weeks and months at home were a blur. Nicholas loved having a playmate available to him all day, every day. Katie watched him wide-eyed and discovered the world as he unwrapped it for her. She didn't initiate play but was a willing participant in his vibrant and imaginative world.

"Come on, Katie, let's go outside. Come on, Katie, let's play Duplos. Come on, Katie ..."

Katie began making sounds and trying to speak after about two months. By then, we realized her issues were more significant than we first thought. She rocked and drooled constantly. Food frequently stuck to the edge of her mouth because she couldn't feel it. Her tongue hung limply to the side unless she was clicking it. Katie's rigid body positions looked awkward. She stared at her fist as if it wasn't attached to her body, straightening her arm and then curling it, nearly hitting her forehead. It was horrifying to see the effects of malnourishment and neglect.

A friend of my mom's loaned me a book called *High-Risk: Children Without a Conscience,* which detailed cases of adopted children who grew into liars, thieves, and psychopaths. It was alarming and discouraging. I didn't know why this woman felt it was appropriate to share it. We'd already adopted our daughter, and the book lacked specific strategies to help high-risk children like Katie.

If I had to take the kids with me to the grocery store, Katie cried much of the time, overwhelmed by the lights and sounds. When other people shot me dirty looks, which I assumed were about my poor parenting, I vacillated between telling them to mind their own business and crying. Regret for those times I'd shot someone a disapproving look filled me, and I vowed to be more compassionate to every parent.

When I dropped Katie off at the church nursery on Sunday mornings, I reminded the gracious volunteers she didn't like being cuddled. She was hypersensitive to touch, and instead of calming her, it sent her body into high alert. They looked at me like I was crazy. They couldn't understand.

That first year, Katie learned how to crawl and eventually walked. She gained ten pounds and grew five inches, and we got into a routine. We secured services through the regional center for speech therapy, occupational therapy, play therapy, and more. At one point, we had people coming into our home five days a week.

One therapist suggested I read a book called *Holding Time* by Martha Welch. It states it's a "breakthrough parenting strategy—a revolutionary approach to mother-child bonding that can make all children happier, more cooperative, and more self-confident." It was a method that involved holding your child closely for an hour each day. The child resisted and struggled but eventually became quiet.

I tried this approach, and it was a battle of who became exhausted first. She fought against me fiercely and cried like I was torturing her. It didn't feel like it was helping, and I figured I was doing something wrong. Not knowing how to do something was not in my repertoire. Nicholas had been such an easy baby and toddler, and any smugness I had about my capable parenting evaporated with Katie.

Katie's diagnoses started piling up—sensory integration issues, speech delays, fetal alcohol exposure, and reactive attachment disorder or RAD—something few people had ever heard of. It is a condition primarily found in neglected and abused children who don't form healthy attachments with their caregivers, typically females. This diagnosis triggered her first referral for mental health services at age three. Most of what I read about RAD was very discouraging. Katie's RAD would never go away with time or love, and any chance for improvement depended on finding good therapists.

Katie and I worked with a nice grandmother-type for attachment-building. We sat on the floor, and the therapist tried to engage Katie and me in pretend play. Katie gazed at the dolls but couldn't create a conversation or mimic any dialogue between a parent and child. When I started the imaginary conversation, she stared back blankly. I looked away, frustrated at the lack of progress. These sessions felt like the definition of insanity—doing the same thing repeatedly and expecting different results, so we stopped.

Chapter Eleven

Every parent blows it. Every kid comes unhinged.
Every family goes off the rails.
That doesn't mean we are ruined.
It means we are ordinary.

Jen Hatmaker, *For the Love*

As the kids grew up, we appeared to be a respectable family of four, living the American dream. People said we'd done an admirable thing by adopting Katie and expressed compassion because of her vast array of issues. When I heard this, guilt made me feel dishonest because I wanted one boy and one girl, like my family growing up. That I helped rescue a child from an orphanage was a bonus.

Katie and Nicholas went to a preschool within walking distance of our house, several days a week. It offered an excellent inclusion program that incorporated children with special needs. It normalized interactions for students of varying abilities instead of stigmatizing them. The teachers even potty-trained Katie when my attempts were unsuccessful.

Katie's fears manifested in strange ways. Paul and I knew she was severely malnourished but didn't understand the extensive impacts until she had been in our home for years. One morning I walked down the hall, and her room smelled rank. When I searched for the source, I found bags of food in various stages of decay under her bed. Given my own issues with being told which foods I could and couldn't eat, I had not been particularly restrictive with my children's consumption. After Katie had intestinal problems related to eating too much cheese, something that led to her nickname "Dairy Mouse," she was limited to a serving or two per day. Because of her ADHD, we also minimized her sugar intake. But we stocked our refrigerator and pantry with plenty of options she could access on her own. The effects of the instability and uncertainty of her first year and a half continued to surprise me. Moving from place to place, with different caregivers, and inconsistent access to food, affects even the youngest children. Her need to have food in her room felt illogical, but I learned it is not uncommon for children from orphanages who lacked any control in their lives.

Katie's issues weren't limited to food, either. She had no fear of strangers and would gladly follow anyone new. We recognized she was vulnerable to strangers wanting to take advantage of her and devised a system. If anyone ever told her that her mom or dad sent them to pick her up, she'd ask for the code word—weasel. If they didn't know it, she wouldn't go with them. The trouble was that we didn't know if she could remember the word.

Parenting two children was much more complex than having one. I texted Paul and told him he'd have one less child if he didn't come home immediately on particularly tough days. He always did because he knew I was losing it when I gave in and asked for support. My mom also helped with weekly babysitting, so I didn't lose my sanity. She had a nice pool next to her house and taught Katie to swim. It turned out to be the place Katie felt most comfortable. The water soothed her sensory issues, and she loved spinning and being tossed in the air.

I felt conflicted as a mother. I loved being Nicholas' mom and all it entailed ... trips to the zoo, endless adventures, sports, and projects. My heart swelled with abundant love when I thought about him. But the same feelings didn't arise when I thought of Katie. Everything was hard. She cried a lot and was discontented with me. I felt terrible and inadequate, embarrassed that I had those feelings. God had undoubtedly made a mistake. *Could I really be the right mother for her?*

My parents babysat so we could have date nights. It was nice to have time away from the kids, but I dreaded any event where alcohol flowed freely, like Paul's work parties. Sitting with the other work wives, I'd see a tipsy Paul from afar, embarrassed as he stumbled around. It upset me but I rationalized that many others also overindulged, so his behavior wasn't unusual. Was it?

As we enrolled Katie for kindergarten, I sent the obligatory letter to the teacher to introduce her. It was hard to be upbeat. Others saw the charming and funny side of Katie. But that was not my experience. After mulling over several drafts, I wrote:

> Katie is an enthusiastic child, well-liked by her preschool teachers. She has some quirky traits that may make it harder for her to make friends. Katie makes some repetitive hand motions and clicks her tongue to soothe herself. She desires to be compliant and can sit for a long time. She likes to work independently on puzzles and coloring. I think you'll find her quite charming.

I wanted to share that she had wildly differing emotions at home, from intense and exuberant to laughing or shrieking. She had entire conversations with herself but couldn't engage in imaginary play. She needed individual attention to follow directions and multiple prompts before transitioning. But if I wrote all of that in the letter, our family wouldn't look so good. I didn't want her to be the problem child no teacher wanted in class. So, I wrote what was accurate enough. It wasn't deceitful, right? I was just trying to protect Katie.

Throughout grade school, Katie had a full-time aide. She was a lifesaver, helping Katie stay on task, transition between classes, navigate social situations, and attend sessions with various specialists. Katie received occupational therapy, sensory integration therapy, adaptive physical education, and speech therapy. The other students accepted her quirks and vocalizations, and the teachers enjoyed having another adult in the classroom to help. Katie was a compliant student and wanted to please the adults at school.

At home, though, I got the worst of her. The school psychologist told me it took all Katie's energy to keep it together at school, so she melted down with me. Not only did Katie have attachment issues, I believed *I* had attachment issues, too. It was hard to feel affection for her, even though I knew her trauma. We didn't have a foundational bond, as I had with Nicholas. With him, our bond allowed me to love him, even when I didn't like his actions. I tried counseling for my lack of attachment with Katie, but it never made me feel better or changed our relationship, so I stopped, feeling lost and hopeless.

I asked other parents if they felt differently about their kids—some did, and some didn't. Others shared phrases like "love is an action." But at the end of each day, parenting Katie felt like an unending babysitting journey from hell. She couldn't go back to Russia, and I couldn't help her. I just wished I felt more compassionate about how hard her life was and the rotten beginning she had. Instead, anger with her and God bubbled within my heart. I wasn't getting the blessed and easy life I expected.

Paul recognized how hard parenting Katie was for me as an overachieving perfectionist. One May, he nominated me for Mother of the Year in a local contest sponsored by a community parent group. It was a generous gesture, but I felt unworthy of the award, even as the runner-up. My head was barely above water, and I certainly wasn't the "Mom of the Year" to Katie. My goal was to be a wonderful, intentional, and loving mother who helped each of them thrive. I worked from home, so my schedule allowed me to volunteer in the classroom and supervise backyard activities like airsoft wars in our treehouse or half-pipe skateboarding.

Nicholas and Katie were close until she was in fifth grade, and he was in sixth. He decided he was now "Nick." He had always been protective of his sister until she and her friend scurried around the playground like animals, making weird sounds. He was embarrassed and distanced himself from her socially unacceptable behaviors.

We planned gatherings they could both enjoy and hosted a back-to-school barbecue with around ten families. Because Nick and Katie were only one grade apart, they knew the same kids, and we enjoyed socializing with their families. The party celebrated the end of summer and reintroduced Katie to peers in an environment over which I had some control. It was always great fun, and the group seemed to enjoy being together.

After one of those parties, I realized I didn't know where Paul was. He should have been helping me clean up.

Instead, he was passed out drunk in front of our fire pit. I turned off the gas line and considered whether to wake him up. He might get hurt if he fell off the chair onto the concrete. But I decided he could endure the natural consequences of his actions, just like the kids did.

Alcohol was a familiar coping mechanism for Paul, and he turned to it more and more, often falling asleep drunk on the couch by 8 p.m. When the kids were young and asked about it, I said he was exhausted from work or running or yard work. As they got older, they stopped asking, so I stopped lying about it.

Once or twice a year on our anniversary or a birthday, he would consciously limit himself to a glass or two of wine, just enough to relax. We'd have a romantic dinner and be intimate afterward. It was the only time I didn't mind his drinking. But I would have given that up in a heartbeat for an alcohol-free household with an engaged partner and father.

My solution to my unhappiness was busyness with activities I could excel at. It balanced the inadequacy I felt. I handled problems and took on more than my share of the workload at home—anything to keep Paul from getting irritated, which would lead to him drinking more. Because my childhood had been so peaceful, his irritation and rage were uncomfortable. The more "off the script" our life got, the more Paul drank, and the more I controlled as much as I could.

We had some enjoyable family times during our summer vacations. Paul and I relaxed without the pressure of work, and our Type A personalities mellowed. Nick and Katie had enjoyed each other and reverted to the friendship they had as younger children. Nick's sarcasm matched ours, but with her autistic characteristics, Katie couldn't comprehend this communication style, so we tried to tone it down around her.

One of the funniest interchanges occurred when they were in grade school. The three of us were at a restaurant, and the server brought me full sugar, not diet soda, which is not good for a person with diabetes.

Katie's eyes grew big, and she asked, "Are you going to die?"

I said, "If I were, what would your last words to me be?"

Katie replied, "I'd say love you."

With a smile on his face, Nick said, "Have a nice trip."

She started crying. "How can you say that to Mom?"

I stifled a laugh but found it hilarious. Katie couldn't understand how Nick's words were funny. It was unusual for Katie to express concern for others. If someone got hurt, Katie would laugh. If someone had a neutral face, she thought they were mad at her. Katie would tell strangers she loved them the first time they met but didn't tell me without prompting until she was in her teens.

Paul and I were like two steam engines running on parallel tracks. We were both driven and determined to appear successful and "normal." Paul worked to support the family, did the yard work, and oversaw our finances. I managed the kids, the household, and excelled at my job and volunteer activities. We got things done, but we were not living.

We asked ourselves the terrible question of whether we'd made a mistake in adopting. We were alone together—the only two people who knew the magnitude of Katie's issues. When we tried to explain it to others, they thought we were overly dramatic and complainers. And we commiserated in that isolation from the world while isolating ourselves from each other through alcohol and busyness.

Then Paul's father passed unexpectedly at sixty-nine years old while fishing in Alaska. Paul fell to the floor when he received the call and cried. He never cried. In fact, he rarely showed any emotion other than anger. Paul had complicated feelings about his father, and I wasn't sure how his death would affect us. I wasn't sure how to support Paul. But I was sure he hadn't said all he needed to say to his dad when he had the chance.

During his dad's funeral, family members lauded him as if he had been a wonderful family man. When he was eulogized for being a great father, I wanted to object, remind them of the drunken escapades they'd witnessed, and to ask what definition of a father he was being measured by. If a great father pushed his child through a plate-glass window and beat him with a belt, then yes, he got an A+. But my definition of a good father was someone who loved his children and mentored them, worked hard, practiced patience and self-control, and was respectable. In that case, Paul's dad was a miserable failure. The family was deceiving themselves about who he was. Unfortunately, the pattern was repeating itself in our family. I just didn't realize it until later.

Chapter Twelve

We must be willing to get rid of the life we've planned,
to have the life that is waiting for us.
The old skin has to be shed before the new one can come.

Joseph Campbell

In Missouri, Katie's therapist at the treatment center assured us she was learning coping skills, but she still struggled with depression and rapidly cycling moods. I could not admit it aloud, but I was learning thankfulness for the journey. If I could shed my perfectionist ways, my core need to help others may be fulfilled. If one person could glean something from our experience, it would be worth it.

The optimistic feelings waned as Katie had a full anxiety attack during a family therapy session by phone. Paul paced in his office while I walked around the parking lot at mine, texting our frustration and feelings of inadequacy throughout. Katie's screaming and crying, the gulping and sniffling, and the whimpering were torture from thousands of miles away, and Paul and I were grateful Katie's therapist was there to handle it.

A few weeks later, as my parents were on their way to visit Katie in Missouri, her therapist called to say Katie had been worsening over the previous twenty-four hours. She was delusional, fearful that everyone was plotting to kill her. She'd been kicking at staff, screaming, and having panic attacks. They wanted to send her to an adolescent psychiatric hospital about ninety minutes away, and we agreed that sounded like the right course of action.

Disappointment flooded me. Katie wouldn't get to do fun activities with my parents, but I was relieved they were there. It felt like some family member should be with her, even though it didn't matter to Katie. The therapist thought Katie might have had a breakdown because she was making progress. When kids with reactive attachment disorder see success, they can become afraid and regress. Lesson learned.

The stress of our lives continued. As usual, Paul drank with his work friends, came home, and passed out on the couch. I sat on the fluffy cream carpet in my cozy walk-in closet, my beautiful clothes hanging by style and color. The rich chocolate brown of my boots contrasted with the white walls that held black and white prints of Nick and Katie as young children. Everything was in its place, and I should have felt at ease because organization provided the reliability and control I craved.

Instead, like so many nights before, I hugged my knees to my chest, my Bible next to me, tears streaming down my face. I searched verses filled with hope but the words I trusted and believed so many times felt hollow. God had not given me the life I expected, or I thought I deserved. My secrets were terrible—too shameful to share. Disappointment and devastation overwhelmed me. My closet was my haven; its clean scent mixed with a hint of leather was oddly comforting. Paul was unlikely to find me when he woke from his blackout, the walls insulating my sobs.

I silently screamed at God while dreading the repercussions of my rage.

I questioned whether I had been "a good (enough) girl." I followed the rules, loved God, and went to church. I didn't have sex before marriage, drink, or use drugs. I didn't beat my children and worked to be the best parent I could be. My self-criticism always centered on the twenty pounds I should lose. But, overall, if I was realistic, I was the total package. What had I done so wrong?

Was there a way to get out of the marriage without getting divorced? I wondered if Paul would ever drive drunk enough to wrap his car around a tree. In my desperate state, his death seemed to be my only way out. I couldn't leave him. Divorce would be yet another sign of failure—my scarlet letter displayed prominently—a symbol I hadn't been perfect enough to earn an easy and blessed life. It seemed my choices were that I could die, he could die, or I could live with the shame of divorce. But something had to happen. I couldn't live in this disaster of a life any longer. Either I had done it wrong, or the formula was wrong. Both were incomprehensible. The unraveling of my life was unbearable.

Two weeks later, Nick, Paul, and I were in our family room. It had been a busy week, and I was looking forward to relaxing. The California Public Information Officials (CAPIO) conference had been in Santa Barbara, and they gave me the highest honor in my profession—Communicator of the Year. What I thought about wasn't the glory of getting the award or the speech I delivered, but that Paul and I fought before the gala about whether he could control his drinking. I didn't want to be embarrassed in front of my colleagues.

So that Friday night, Good Friday, it was no surprise Paul was passed out on the couch. A movie played on television while Nick sat nearby, working on the family computer. Paul woke up, disoriented, and looked at his phone. He threw it across the room a moment later and stomped upstairs to retrieve his work computer, mumbling. Paul complained he always had to be the responsible one, solving problems at work. He plopped back down on the couch, opened his laptop, and then threw it, shocking me. While life irritated him regularly, he rarely acted out. Nick went upstairs to his room, and I stayed in the family room, paralyzed and unable to figure out what to do.

Sometimes I tried to talk to Paul rationally and asked, "Is anyone going to die today because of this call/email/fill in the blank?" to give perspective. But I stayed silent this time and watched as his forehead creased and his face turned red. He shoved the chair Nick had been sitting on, said a few choice words to no one in particular, grabbed his car keys, and slammed the front door.

My life would never be the same. I finally acknowledged what I had been unwilling to consider—Paul had a serious problem with alcohol. It was no longer safe for me to pretend he didn't. It was as if I'd been holding my breath for years and finally exhaled.

As soon as the door slammed, Nick came downstairs. I couldn't speak for a few moments, massaging my temples and thinking about the magnitude of this moment. A word or two came from my lips, but then I stopped, swallowing hard, knowing if I continued, tears would pour out. I had to be strong for Nick. I was always the strong one, the parent who held it together, and I feared that if he saw me crumble, he would fall apart, too.

After calming myself, we talked on the stairs for a long time. Nick was much more aware of the unspoken words, chaos, and dysfunction in our home than I realized. One minute Paul tried to be the cool dad, and the next, he was stumbling and cussing at no one in particular. Nick had stopped inviting friends over because of Paul's erratic behavior, which upset Nick. He wasn't comfortable in our home. Now that he was older and taller, he was ready to stand up for himself and me. In my attempt to protect him, I had taught him lying was acceptable, making various excuses for Paul over the years.

Something in me snapped that night. I'd had enough and told Nick I planned to ask Paul to move out the next day.

At nearly six feet tall and sixteen years old, Nick said he'd protect me from whatever would happen with Paul. While Paul never physically hurt me, he was menacing when intoxicated, and I didn't know how he'd react to my request.

Nick hugged me and said he loved me.

Crying through the night, I asked myself: *Why did you think you could pretend this wasn't happening? The kids weren't stupid. They saw their dad drunk on the couch. Other dads didn't behave that way. Why did I cover for him so often?*

My entire life was based on the formula—be perfect, do good, love God—yet it hadn't worked out how I thought it would.

In previous years, Paul and I had stopped socializing. All he wanted to do was relax, which was code for drinking a few martinis or a bottle of wine. As my circle of friends diminished, my isolation grew. I couldn't share my personal hell. It would reflect poorly on us because "people in the church didn't struggle with alcohol." If Paul had cancer, we would have found lots of support. But alcoholism was a moral failure and a fatal character defect, and I didn't have one person I could tell.

A few times, I tried to control the alcohol in our house by pouring the vodka out or adding water to the bottle, trying to fool him. But it felt stupid pouring our money down the drain. I tried the approach of just not buying it, but if I didn't, he became irritated, and I was reluctant to confront him. He was intimidating at 6'1" to my 5'4". So, I kept buying it to avoid conflict.

Instead, I controlled everything else. If I was perfect enough—thin, pretty, intelligent, organized, the ideal homemaker, and PTA rockstar, I would be more lovable, and he would stop drinking, right? I did diet and exercise programs, was a super volunteer, led mom groups, and won professional awards. I pressured myself to perform because that was the only way I felt worthy, but it created stress and didn't change his behavior.

I thought back to one night where, after an evening of drinking, he urinated on the hardwood floor in front of our closet as he got undressed.

"What are you doing? Are you crazy? Gosh. Clean it up!"

He was surprised by my yelling and cleaned it up before passing out on the bed.

Once I sought the help of a Christian counselor, believing she would offer an acceptable solution since we shared the same faith. Any non-Christian therapist would take my side and recommend divorce, but that was unacceptable. Instead of helping me figure out how to change Paul, this counselor, in recovery herself, said, "It sounds like your husband is an alcoholic." She handed me a copy of *Codependent No More* and an Al-Anon brochure. I bawled as I left her office and said there was no way I was going to meetings for his problem.

It was the first time the idea of Paul being an alcoholic had ever occurred to me. Because he was very high functioning at work, I never considered he could be an alcoholic. Weren't alcoholics dirty, smelly, homeless men begging for money on the street corners with their grubby hands?

The night I met with the counselor, I asked Paul to walk around the neighborhood with me thinking he'd have to control his temper if we were in a public place. When I mentioned the therapist's words, he was defensive, arguing about how hard his life was and why he needed alcohol to help him unwind from the stress. The conversation went nowhere. At home, I retreated to my office, and he went to bed—our well-worn pattern of coping with life.

The co-dependency book made me cringe. How had I, the confident, independent college student who wanted to save the world, become a controlling, cowering, isolated, sad human? I was a good person, a smart individual, a confident woman who had grown up in a great family. As a young girl, I'd heard everyone got what they deserved, like the man who died after stealing from our church. Poor decisions caused family problems. Uncommitted or undisciplined people who lacked character got divorced. Imagine my shame from all those years of having a "troubled" and difficult life. I hadn't caused it. I wasn't weak-willed, and I hadn't made bad choices, but here I was.

That Good Friday evening, Paul never came home ... a first. Relieved and terrified, I finally fell asleep. The following day, he texted and asked if he could come over to talk. Ten minutes later, Nick and I met him in the driveway. He apologized and was contrite. But I told him to gather his things and move out immediately, which he did without making a scene.

After he left, I inhaled, trying to calm and fortify myself for the unpleasant task of telling my parents. It was a conversation I needed to have with them in person. My hands were shaking as I drove two miles to their house and knocked unannounced. They knew something was very, very wrong when they opened the door but assumed it was Katie. We sat in their living room, and I unraveled the story of the life I'd hidden from everyone.

Tears filled my parents' eyes, shocked at what the kids and I lived through. Describing the years of trauma was hard because it was still uncomfortable to share the dark secrets that had kept me isolated and alone. Mom and Dad learned about the events we skipped because I feared Paul would be a drunk or a jerk, and the times I lied to them about Paul being sick while throwing up in our front yard. They were heartbroken I hadn't felt I could come to them for support.

Later that day, Paul asked me to go to see a family therapist with him. Expecting little, I agreed, figuring if I went, no one could criticize me for not trying to work out our problems. We saw the therapist the next afternoon, and the session centered on Paul's drinking. We'd worked with this therapist before, so she knew the dynamics of our life. She connected Paul with someone in Alcoholics Anonymous. But absolute clarity came when he asked if I would take him back if he stopped drinking

I said, "… not until you figure out who you are."

That phrase was a neon sign flickering in my brain. Something was off, but I hadn't been able to name it. Paul was a chameleon. When he didn't reek of alcohol at church, he served on committees and was an excellent pianist. At work, he was a high-strung, top performer known for getting things done. When his company needed him to close a deal in China, he could drink with the best of them. But his identity, who he was at his core, eluded him.

While I dreaded the unraveling of my life, I could no longer bear the burden of our marriage. Separating was the right thing. Four months later, Paul and I were at the mediator, working out the details of our divorce settlement. As the first person in my family to get divorced, I felt like a black sheep and complete failure.

Chapter Thirteen

Life has many ways of testing a person's will, either by having nothing happen at all or by having everything happen at once.

Paulo Coelho

Two weeks after Paul moved out, we had one of our weekly family phone therapy sessions with Katie. We'd already told her therapist we were separated and strategized about how to tell Katie. The day we shared the news, Katie was more compassionate toward Paul because "he was sick and drank too much alcohol." She related to that because she, too, was sick. Katie felt like they were both underdogs, and he needed her support. As a typical child with reactive attachment disorder, she was most resistant to the primary caregiver, me. At the end of the therapy session, we told her we'd see her the following week at the retreat, which helped her calm down a little.

It was unusual for Paul and me to travel together because we alternated our visits, so Katie saw one of us every six or eight weeks. But during this trip, we were on the same flights and talked while we walked to kill time during our two layovers.

I was curious about how he was doing with the drinking. But he came right out and told me he'd been sober since the day I asked him to move out. Paul described how he connected with some people in Alcoholics Anonymous, and they encouraged him to attend one hundred meetings in one hundred days. He had gotten a sponsor and began working the twelve steps. He talked excitedly about what he had learned about himself and seemed to have a new perspective on life. Two things stuck out. He wished his ego hadn't prevented him from asking for help from my dad, who he saw as a model father and husband. Paul realized he could have learned so much from him. Then he said I had likely saved his life because his drinking had gotten progressively worse over the years. Paul said he probably wouldn't have stopped without me kicking him out. I was surprised and pleased he didn't paint me as the bad guy. It was good he was working through the issues that drove him to drink and I was happy to be out of the role of monitoring his alcohol consumption.

Once we finally arrived at the retreat center, Katie acted relieved Paul and I were getting along well as if nothing had happened. We did a mask-making activity to promote appropriate, intimate touch, something Katie had never enjoyed or wanted. We applied wet newspaper strips to

Katie's face and laughed, uncomfortable with the closeness, something we'd not experienced very often as a family.

Next, we wrote characteristics of the ideal self on one side of our papers and positive adjectives describing ourselves on the other. Katie, the little girl who had been in speech therapy since her feet reached California, read her list aloud in front of the group of twenty. The other students praised her for not becoming overwhelmed.

When I arrived home after the retreat, I exhaled, pleased to have conquered our first co-parenting experience with relative ease. Katie was safe. Paul was finding himself. And Nick and I were beginning to heal. Tension eased from my shoulders, and I slept better. It felt more comfortable between Nick and me. We'd always spent more time together than any other combination of people in the house. I gladly drove him to surf when the waves were good, or to a new skate park when he wanted to try one out. It had always been that way between us. Back in second grade, he had been invited to be in a commercial for a new ride at Magic Mountain. I said, "Let's go!" When he had wanted to learn guitar, I signed him up for lessons. His best friend called me Mom, and his girlfriend hung out and talked with me at the kitchen counter. I thought I was a pretty cool parent, with a special bond with Nick.

Nick was glad Paul and I finally separated. He told me he thought we would get divorced after he and Katie finished high school. But there was no point in pretending any longer. While Paul and I didn't fight, there was constant tension in our marriage. We were two high-strung individuals to start. When the magnitude of Katie's issues emerged, we were like landmines waiting to explode. The difference was that Paul's fuse was short. He got mad and got over it. My fuse could burn for years without incident and then blow up. I think that's what happened the night I decided he needed to move out.

Paul had taken most of his things within a few weeks. He wanted almost nothing except his grand piano, and I donated anything else I considered his. One night, I decided the stemware and martini glasses needed to go. Rather than selling them on Craigslist, I figured it would be much more fun and therapeutic to smash them. I asked Nick if he wanted to join me. He looked at me like I was crazy but said sure. We lifted the recycling bin cover in the garage and started hurling glass after glass as hard as possible. It felt inappropriate, something a "good girl" wouldn't do, but it was cathartic. Nick seemed to enjoy the release of tension, too, with his budding anger issues. It was another way for me to eliminate the evidence of a life gone awry.

The shame of divorce after almost nineteen years of marriage was painful. I was plagued with thoughts that there must have been something I could have done better. Feelings of imperfection, incompetence, and perceived judgment from others saturated my mind.

Then there was the practical side of figuring out how to do everything—from managing my finances to making ends meet by renting out one of our five bedrooms. Paul had been a stable provider, but we didn't have an intimate and emotional connection, both of us with our blind spots. While I missed the financial stability, I enjoyed the peace and predictability of our days. I no longer had to wonder if he would be testy with us or if I could count on him for help. I didn't have to buy alcohol, ever, and I didn't have to wash sweaty bedsheets that reeked of alcohol or clean up his literal and figurative messes.

Nick completed his sophomore year but wasn't unscathed by the life-changing events of the previous twelve months. He was moody, and I hoped it was just the strain and not something more significant. I'd been so focused on Katie's case management and trying to mitigate Paul's stress that I'd checked out on parenting Nick.

I missed the confident and secure boy he had been. Nick was the kid unfazed by wearing his penguin costume to school on Halloween. On trips to the shopping center, he and his friends made funny expressions and put on girdles and children's bike helmets, just for entertainment. Those were the times I missed. His laughter bubbling over, and the feeling he was doing okay.

Because I lacked the finesse to talk with Nick about feelings, I wrote him a note. Writing had always been my way of processing life. But it was also my cowardly attempt at saying what I needed to say without seeing the reaction.

Years earlier, when I wrote about how to treat girls, his eye roll said everything I needed to know.

> Dear Nick,
>
> When I say yes to driving you and your buddy to surf Jalama Beach, which requires me to get up at 6 a.m. on a weekend morning, you think it's cool, but I call it love. When I take you to Starbucks at 9:55 p.m. on a school night or make you and your friends pancakes and bacon, it's love. That's the same love with which I occasionally say no.
>
> I'm not perfect and don't expect you to be. In fact, I want you to fail. Yep, you read that correctly. I want you to have experiences where everything isn't perfect so that you develop the life skills needed to handle disappointments and difficult situations later. However, I want you to do it while you're still living at home as a minor. Trust me. I will be much more loving than a Sheriff's deputy.
>
> It has been an extraordinarily tough year for our family, and you get an A+ in resiliency. Someday you can read "David & Goliath" by Malcolm Gladwell and the chapter about resiliency. He's a much better writer than I am and articulates this meaningfully. The lessons you've learned unknowingly will serve you

> well as you journey through the rest of your life. I would never wish our past year on anyone, but we have to be grateful for the growth opportunities it has provided.
>
> So, I am going to keep on loving you how I do. And yes, I'll be uncool, but hopefully, you'll understand when you're the parent of a teen.

I hoped he'd understand that I was doing my best, and I was showing him love in the ways I knew how. I planned a week-long vacation with his best friend to San Clemente, with its awesome surf breaks. They'd surf and skate, and I'd take lots of pictures and videos of them, which they loved. Everything was going to be okay, wasn't it?

It had been a year since the junior high graduation Katie couldn't attend. I grieved, missing the milestones my friends and their families enjoyed. I tried to share in their delight but felt a profound sense of loss at the moments I didn't get to experience.

Adding to this mix of emotions was Katie's anger about the divorce and her general emotional state. She worried about how a split would affect her home life. Which home would she live in? Who would be the primary parent? She asked questions to which we didn't have answers. We assured her we loved her and were trying to do what was healthy for all of us.

Katie was angry with the other girls in her home, too, frequently screaming that they were trying to hurt her when she was the one grabbing them aggressively. She would overreact to them and then accuse them of harming her. When Katie wasn't getting the attention she craved, she'd hit her head against a concrete wall or try to smother herself in her blankets. When they took them away, she claimed they were abusing her. For her safety, and that of the other students, Katie couldn't take part in off-campus activities, like a visit to a zoo or their annual camping trip. She was too erratic. None of her therapies seemed to be working well enough, and her doctor couldn't find the sweet spot with medication.

A new program for younger girls opened up, and the staff thought Katie would be more successful in that group. While she was fifteen, she acted more like a ten-year-old. They thought if she felt less threatened, she might calm down. It was definitely worth trying.

Katie liked the new team but was furious she hadn't been able to move home. Girls who had come in after her were leaving. She thought she had earned the right to go home permanently. But Katie was not like other girls. While her IQ was high, her emotional understanding was virtually non-existent. I questioned if she would ever understand herself and others.

In October, I visited Katie again, making the long journey with three flights and three and one-half hours of driving. Going to the middle of nowhere to spend time with a daughter with whom I had no attachment was not a vacation. My emotional tank was always on empty when I arrived, which made the visits more challenging.

Katie introduced me to Carsen, her golden retriever, and, for the first time, we remained in the group home for a few minutes with her teammates. As Carsen showed off her tricks, the girls were friendly. This home with younger girls didn't have the negative flow of her previous one.

Carsen and Katie bonded. We walked her by the lake, and Carsen followed several ducks into the water. We yelled her name, coaxing her to come toward the dock, but she didn't respond, and Katie grew concerned for her. Excellent swimmer that she was, Katie jumped in to help. Her affection and concern for Carsen were endearing. Most of the parenting journey with Katie had been a slog. Nothing like I envisioned. So I treasured any enjoyable moment.

A few weeks later, incident reports increased. Katie had bitten a peer, kicked her staff, and snarled like an animal, terrifying another student. They found disturbing notes in her binder.

"I don't wanna work anymore. I just wanna die. I'm tired of living, and I have sleeping problems. I should just die."

Another said, "I cannot kill myself, but I am scared too, so I want someone else to kill me. I wish I could be shot in the head so I could die quick, and it would not hurt."

It was unending, and I asked them to stop notifying me. I couldn't deal with it. I dreaded the weekly phone calls between Katie and me and the family therapy sessions with Paul, Katie, and the therapist. Katie wasn't progressing. The psychiatrist diagnosed her with autism spectrum disorder after the previous placement ruled it out, and we were back on the game show of "pick your diagnoses."

We had our fall teleconference with various support staff from the school district and the treatment facility to discuss Katie's progress. To prepare for each meeting, the speech therapist, occupational therapist, and school psychologist wrote goals like "take part in a ten-minute structured conversation in which she appropriately participates—asking and responding to the other person" and "keep binder organized eighty-five percent of the time." It felt ridiculous, given all she wanted to do was die. But the school had to track it to continue to fund this program. If she was actually meeting the goals, it wouldn't have felt as awful.

During one of our individual calls, Katie said, "I've made as much progress as I can. I think I need a new place. Even if I can't take Carsen, it's okay. I need to do my work."

Wow. The comment showed terrific insight, highly unusual for Katie. Most of the time, she couldn't remember anything, let alone have insight. But occasionally, she'd come out with a zinger. Paul and I texted about it, as she had told him the same thing. We agreed to the move but dreaded the process.

The treatment team had also realized Katie had gotten everything she could from her current placement. The district's facilitator began the challenging process of looking for a place to balance Katie's immaturity and low social skills with her higher-than-average intelligence. Because Katie's needs were so unique with autism, reactive attachment disorder, mood and anxiety disorders, fetal alcohol syndrome, sensory integration issues, and more, I was grateful this person was leading the way, and I didn't have to be in charge.

Chapter Fourteen

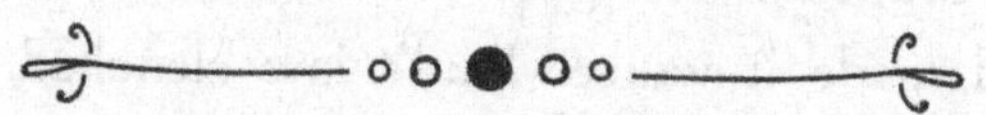

This is not who you are. This happened to you, but it does not define you. You are not broken. You are not ruined. You are not destined for a lifetime of sexual dysfunction. You will become the exact person God intended all along, and you will be stronger in these fragile places than you were before it happened. This is a part of your story, not the end of it, and you will overcome. Not only that; you will thrive.

Jen Hatmaker, *Of Mess and Moxie*

As Thanksgiving approached, I knew the holiday season would be different. It was my first Christmas as a divorced parent and my second with Katie thousands of miles away. While I dreaded the holidays under these circumstances, I loved them, too—the music, baking, tree trimming, and gift wrapping. For too many years, I'd fabricated a joyful family life. I wished I'd had the guts to send the actual photos depicting our lives as I looked back.

When the kids were young, we scheduled a session at the nearest Sears Photo Studio. My mom made Katie a beautiful green velvet dress with a red plaid blouse. Nick had on a cute sweater with a red fire truck, and Paul and I coordinated with them. The photographer positioned Katie on my lap, and she started crying, not feeling comfortable being that close. Then the photographer's assistant draped a string of red ornaments around her neck and made it worse. Paul's jaw clenched, and my shoulders bunched up around my neck while Nick tried to soothe her. We felt guilty for the family drama we put the photographer through and bought a package of the most horrible pictures, even though we knew we'd never send them. In subsequent years, we bribed the kids and faked the smiles.

It was a relief to no longer pretend. My life had burst apart, which was awful. But over the previous months, I read and listened to a lot of material that helped me discover that authenticity, not perfection, was what I craved. Once I tasted the freedom imperfection provided, I didn't want to return to my old ways, joyful as I shed the unhealthy aspects of my life. One of my friends, who I hadn't seen for about eight months, said, "You look so much lighter — physically, emotionally, *and* spiritually …" And I felt it. An enormous weight had lifted. My word for the year had been hope. While it didn't transpire as expected, I looked forward to the upcoming year of opportunity. I was ready to meet the new and improved version of myself.

Eight months after I kicked Paul out, I went on a beach walk with a close friend. During our conversation, she said she thought I should start dating. I drew back in dismay at the suggestion. *Really?* I didn't know the unspoken protocol on this sort of stuff. *Was I going to date again? Was I ready to date? I enjoyed being married, but was I open to getting remarried? How would I know I wasn't making another colossal mistake?*

Looking back, I definitely wouldn't have married Paul had I known he would become an alcoholic. But we had been in love, and he checked all my boxes, as did I for him. We were only twenty-three and twenty-four, and neither of us knew enough about ourselves back then. I applied the exact formula I observed in my parents' marriage and figured it would work out.

But my friend was right. I needed to get out of my cave. Eight months of "singleness" plus multiple years of feeling alone in my marriage was enough. My New Year's resolution was to be open-minded about the possibility of dating. But once she planted the idea, I went home and started browsing dating sites and signed up for two. The questions asked were fun to answer, and it was interesting and exciting to consider the more in-depth responses.

Who am I? What did I need? What did I want? Did I want to date casually or be in a committed relationship? How would I describe myself and my ideal mate?

They didn't teach post-divorce marketing in college. After all, I couldn't write:

> "Cute, forty-something with an exciting career seeks wonderful Christian guy. Must be intelligent, funny, willing to do dishes. Must be college educated and gainfully employed with all of his teeth. Cannot be an alcoholic or insecure. Must adore me and accept my kids, realizing that my daughter's situation will require lifelong parenting. Must understand that sometimes I need to not be strong. I'm not overly emotional or weak, but I am human.

It was a challenge to remember what my hobbies were. Did supporting a special needs daughter, trauma, travel, and surf photography count? Advocating, chauffeuring, and caring for my children had taken all my time. Instead of those honest remarks, I wrote something I thought was intriguing. I found a few flattering pictures, hit the "get started" button, and waited. Within minutes, I started getting messages. It was flattering and entertaining.

A 28-year-old wrote, *"You're gorgeous. I'd like to get to know you."*

I laughed aloud and knew what he wanted.

"Thank you. You realize you are closer in age to my son than to me, right?"

"I like older women."

"I'm not interested in dating men that young."

"We can be friends."

"I have lots of friends."

"I live in Goleta."

"That's the worst pickup line I've ever heard."

"You're right. Have a good day."

On the other end, a 70-year-old messaged me about baking him an apple pie.

I embraced online dating as if it were my job. Fear and insecurity would not handcuff me. Even though I hadn't dated a lot when I was younger, I felt confident in who I had become. I was more poised, self-assured, and felt better in my own skin.

Within two weeks, one man, JR, and I had talked on the phone several times. We had a good connection, and I enjoyed our conversations. In my dating discomfort, I tried to set him up with a co-worker first because they were both into dancing. I was as graceful as an elephant and told him so. But he pursued me, and we agreed to meet for lunch in a quaint town midway between our homes. I had a public job and knew many people in my community, and I was not ready for the world to know. Even though no one was interested in my love life, I didn't want to hear feedback from anyone who thought I should wait longer or focus on my kids.

First impressions were essential, and I picked a cute outfit to go with my favorite boots. JR showed up in frumpy dad jeans and white tennis shoes with a baseball cap to protect his new hair implants. I had nothing against bald heads, but his outfit screamed *dad bod*.

We had a pleasant lunch, but he kept cozying up to me. He wasn't picking up on the fact I wasn't feeling attracted to him. As we walked around the village, he asked me what I thought about us.

Is this really happening on a FIRST DATE?

Fumbling around for kind words, I eventually said, "I think we can be friends, but I'm just not feeling the chemistry."

My friend laughed when I called her with my first date story on my way home.

A few weeks later, Paul texted and asked to come over. We communicated regularly, mostly about parenting Katie, and for a divorced couple, we got along well. We mediated our divorce in two sessions, and the couple who facilitated it, a therapist and an attorney, were surprised at how collaborative we were. We respected each other and wanted the best for our children. So, when Paul texted about coming over, it was no big deal. When he said he had something to tell me, I knew what it was. It was an unusual flash of insight. There had been one other occasion in which I had this same sense. The day he proposed, I intuitively knew what was coming. The same feeling hit me that January afternoon as I waited for him to knock on the front door.

Instead, the door to the garage opened. Nick came in, said hello. He seemed in a hurry to get to his room as if he was running away from something. Paul followed immediately, which surprised me. I didn't know they had been together. I closed the door between the kitchen and hall so Nick wouldn't hear our conversation. Paul said, "I wanted you to know I've been dating. I found someone I like, and it's a guy." He explained he never cheated on me with either a man or a woman.

Without missing a beat, I responded, "I'm not surprised, and I'm happy for you."

A look of relief crossed his face. It must have been very difficult for him to share this with me, and I'm sure that was not the response he expected, given our religious experience in which being gay was unequivocally wrong. I'm grateful I had that moment of clarity to offer compassion and kindness

"Should we tell Nick?" I asked.

"I already did," he replied.

"How did he respond?"

"He didn't say much. I don't know that he knew what to say," Paul replied.

I was upset he hadn't included me in that conversation. Nick had been through enough, and I thought it was something we should have consulted with a family therapist about. But now that we were divorced, I didn't get to give input on how he shared a very personal piece of information with his son.

Nick wasn't surprised. Years ago, he'd said to me, "If Dad weren't married to you, I'd think he was gay."

Um. Okay. What do you do with that?

Paul had always been what I would call metrosexual—which I would describe as meticulous about his grooming and appearance. He was an excellent pianist with little interest in sports. But I thought that made him cultured. I sometimes wondered about the frequency of our physically intimate experiences. Shouldn't he have wanted sex more than once or twice a year? I figured it was the alcohol that made him uninterested, or I wasn't attractive enough. I wished I could have asked a married friend for some perspective at the time. But there had been no one safe enough to share that I thought my husband might be gay.

Earlier, Paul couldn't have acknowledged his feelings. He, too, was living under "good Christian" expectations. His parents were involved in their church, and his dad, a close-minded, racist redneck, would have disowned him if he ever found out. Paul's drinking had helped me deny my feelings about his sexuality because I attributed every odd thing to the drinking instead of looking at what was in front of me.

My co-worker was the only person I could even broach the subject with. Because she was free of religious judgment and a neutral party, I felt I could hint at it.

When I danced around the topic, she said, "Valerie, people make agreements of all sorts to stay married."

She told me the story of her friend whose husband came out after they had children. They agreed to stay married for their kids. But they had an agreement. We did not.

Back when we first separated, people asked if we were going to counseling and a whole slew of questions that weren't their business. It felt like I was being bombarded and was relieved when people learned he was an alcoholic because then I wasn't at fault. But I still felt a lot of judgment from those in our church circles.

When Paul came out, seventy-five percent of the people in our lives weren't surprised, and the other twenty-five percent were utterly shocked. There was something about him that made people wonder. Perhaps it was his attention to detail in his clothes, shoes, and grooming. It wasn't his voice or his mannerisms. It was just a vibe that he could have gone either way. When we were married, I was his heterosexuality identity badge. As the news traveled, the questions decreased, except for the most critical one: "Did you know?"

Of course I didn't know. If I had known, I certainly wouldn't have married him.

Early on, I remember sitting in our first home, the condominium we purchased around our first anniversary. Somehow, a conversation started and veered into uncomfortable territory as Paul spoke about being touched by another boy when he was younger. Paul quickly said it was an innocent childhood thing. He was attracted to women, me, his wife, but felt he should tell me. From my innocent perspective, it seemed like something he should have discussed in our pre-marital counseling. But I accepted him at this word, just like I had with the drinking. I trusted him but later realized we kept a lot of secrets.

I was so naïve. My parents met at their church youth group when my mom was a freshman in high school, and my dad was a senior. They got married at eighteen and twenty-two. I followed five years later, and Brian came nineteen months after that. They loved God, each other, and their families. Fifty-plus years later, they still had a wonderful, fulfilling marriage, just as their parents had before them. That's what I wanted and thought I had committed to when Paul proposed twenty years earlier.

Chapter Fifteen

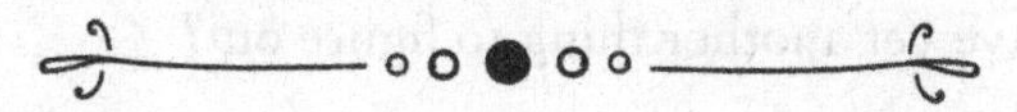

Faith is the strength by which a shattered world shall emerge into the light.

Helen Keller

That spring, I went to a church service to learn more about Lent and resolved to give up bitterness, self-pity, and a sense of entitlement and replace them with joy. It took discipline not to feel sorry for myself. The mind taming was more demanding than any physical task I'd ever attempted.

When I returned home, I checked Paul's Facebook page to see if he posted anything about his visit with Katie. I usually kept his page hidden and only saw his posts when I was emotionally prepared. I found nothing about Katie, just pictures with his new boyfriend. While I didn't feel jealous, it still hurt. How our lives had changed was stretching me in uncomfortable ways. I didn't enjoy being part of a modern and non-traditional family.

I was glad Paul had found peace with himself and wished him the best. He would always be my children's father. He was the only person who truly understood the challenges of raising Katie. And we shared nearly twenty years of married life. But it messed with my mind and made me question myself. While I didn't make him gay, it felt like I must have had some part in it. Why did he choose me? What made a gay guy attracted to a heterosexual woman? Did I have yet another thing to figure out?

With these questions about myself and my path, I started feeling cracks in my faith, believing that life shouldn't be so harsh. I thought I'd healed from much of the parenting trauma but knew I needed to get away from the black and white thinking of should and should not. It was poisoning my mind. Just because I hoped things would be different didn't change what was. I knew acceptance was the key to ending suffering. Still, life shouldn't be so painful.

I'd tried to maintain my faith in God. Over the years, I had seen some miracles, but nothing recently. I didn't feel the comfort and refuge that the Bible promised. I wondered if I still trusted God and believed the phrases church people said—like God will never give you more than you could handle; He was a loving God; He had a plan to prosper me and not to harm me. At that moment, it felt like a bunch of malarky.

So, some days, going to church was excruciating, and on one of those days, my pastor's theme was "Choose Better." I wanted to scream. I chose better, and what did I have to show for it but an unrelenting, painful life? I knew God didn't owe me anything, but I didn't find peace and serenity in the God of my childhood. I no longer had the patience, faith, or perseverance to continue.

Maybe there was a plan for my life. But I didn't like it. I felt pretty beat up. While I was grateful I had become a more compassionate, authentic person, I had reached my limit. If God were my boyfriend, I'd have broken up with him. He had not been meeting my needs.

As I came out of the fog of parenting Katie and being newly single, I realized I had neglected Nick. I hadn't abandoned him—he had everything he needed but my attention. Nick had stopped playing soccer, a disappointment because I loved anything that felt like a typical mom experience. It was a reprieve from the very unusual experience of parenting Katie. But when Nick said he didn't love it, I didn't force him to continue. He still had healthy activities like surfing, biking, and skating that he regularly did with friends.

I hoped he would put more effort into his schoolwork so he would have decent college opportunities. He had so much potential but couldn't seem to pull it all together, and I didn't blame him. It had been a rough few years. It must have been so difficult for him to lose connection with Katie. They adored each other as little kids. But she had been out of state for two years, and they rarely communicated. What was there to talk about? I could imagine their conversations.

"Hi, Katie."

"Hi."

"How are you?"

"Not good."

"What's going on?"

"The girls are being mean."

"Why are the girls being mean?"

"I don't know."

"I'm sorry. I miss you."

"I miss you, too. I just want to die. Can I die? Can you make me stop breathing? Would you miss me if I died?"

Katie would start crying. The staff would grab the phone and tell Nick Katie was done. At least, that's how I thought their conversations might go. She had a limited ability to communicate her feelings and didn't want to admit she was doing anything enjoyable. Nick didn't want to rub in that he was at home, where she wanted to be. Of course, he, too, was struggling. He couldn't even talk to her about that because her interpretation of the world was so different.

His sister was in treatment. His mom and dad recently divorced, and his dad came out as gay. What sixteen-year-old boy wouldn't have a hard time with all that? While Paul and Nick had never been close, it had to be disconcerting when your parent was not what they pretended to be for your entire life.

As the weeks passed, his grades plummeted, and the assistant principal called us into the office to discuss Nick's truancy. I almost laughed at the absurdity of the situation as we sat around the table with representatives from the school and the District Attorney's office. If only they could see the landscape of our lives at that moment—it was a miracle Nick showed up for school at all.

It had been six months since the treatment team concluded Katie should move, and the district still hadn't found an appropriate place. Katie regressed every day—she was deeply depressed, regularly expressing suicidal thoughts. She was angry that Paul and I hadn't found something for her. Her current facility no longer invested in her since she could leave at any moment. It was no way to live. I imagined it was like waiting for a kidney transplant. Every day that passed was one day closer to death. If Katie had the opportunity, she would have taken her life.

After assessing two new facilities and testing Katie, the school district liaison recommended Katie go to a school in Utah for students with autism. We agreed and signed the paperwork

Katie dreaded saying goodbye to her therapist and the dog she had hoped to adopt. She knew she needed different treatment more than she needed her dog, so she let another student adopt him. It was nice to see she had some feelings of attachment. But Paul and I knew her sadness was less about the loss of connection with the dog and therapist and more about the anxiety of moving yet again.

Paul flew to Missouri one last time to pick Katie up. The staff put together a lovely going-away ceremony for her. Given the reports we had received, we were sure it thrilled the students and staff to see her leave. I hoped she would do better at this new place.

Paul brought Katie back to Santa Barbara before she moved to Utah. It was consistent with her previous visits—some enjoyable moments and others that were harder. They always started well when she was excited to leave whatever group home she was in and got progressively worse each day, as she could not hold it together. Weirdly, this was a blessing because it reminded me why she needed to be in a therapeutic boarding school. I questioned whether Katie could do more than she let on since she seemed to perform for short periods. The question that floated around in my head was whether she did or didn't have the capacity to do more.

My parents and I drove Katie to Provo, Utah. I appreciated the help because I never knew how she'd behave. Most of the time, she played her video games and seemed content. But on the night we arrived, Katie had a panic attack in the hotel room we were sharing with my parents. She screamed so loud I feared someone would call the police. I pulled her out of the room into the car, where she raged and cried. I cried, too. We shared in the hopelessness. Even after all this time, I still did not know how to calm her, and I felt inadequate as a mother. It was hard to persevere as we headed to her fourth school in two years.

The school and location were beautiful, set at the base of Utah's Wasatch mountains. Katie was so lethargic and depressed, she barely made it through the tour. If she had been lighter, I would have picked her up and carried her. The stop at the equestrian center was the only time Katie half-smiled. She loved horses and looked forward to riding again. The rest of the time, she dragged her body around the campus for as long as she could. But her anxiety was too high. We said goodbye as she laid on the sensory room floor, moaning and crying. At least the staff witnessed the true Katie and knew what they were getting into. I couldn't wait to escape. My parents and I turned around and headed home. It was an exhausting twenty-four hours of driving over two and a half days.

Five weeks after I left Katie on the sensory room floor at the school, Paul and I discussed whether she should stay there. She was not living with her team because of her threatening behaviors and emotional reactions to other people. She said horrible things to the other girls and acted like a feral cat. We received incident reports daily and sometimes twice per day. Getting them was like hearing from the principal that your child had tried to bite, stab, or kick a peer or staff member. Nothing therapeutic was happening. They were simply keeping her alive. It was inconceivable to think about moving her again. I wondered if there was any place on earth that could help her.

Over the next few weeks, the incident reports eventually decreased. Paul and I didn't know if she'd accepted her new home or the new medication had begun to work. Either way, it felt like a short reprieve from the roller-coaster. We never knew from day to day or even hour to hour what she would be like. Eventually, Paul, Katie, her new therapist, and I had another therapy call, but it wasn't excruciating this time. Katie's mood had flipped, and she was upbeat, talking about horseback riding and swimming. She said she loved this new school. It felt contrived. Katie sometimes faked it to show she was improving while her day-to-day life painted a different picture.

She started swimming and horseback riding, two of her favorite activities. Soon after, I experienced one of the best social calls we'd ever had. She was chatty and shared several concepts she was learning in her program—humor and how to engage in conversation. She tested her skills with girls from another team and felt good about it. It was so refreshing to hear some levity in her voice. One step forward.

A few weeks later, I went home in the middle of the day to pick up something and found Nick and his friends smoking pot in the backyard.

"What are you guys doing? Go back to school. But Nick, you stay. We need to talk."

I suppose I knew Nick had been smoking weed. I gave him the benefit of the doubt when I smelled skunks. *Do we have a lot of skunks? Did someone else hit one on the road again?* It was plausible, at least in my mind, that we had a large skunk population, given our backyard faced an orchard. But I was lying to myself again, unwilling to consider that there was another situation to deal with.

We spoke briefly, then Nick sped away, upset I'd embarrassed him in front of his friends and frustrated I caught them. I headed to the school to see that he returned but passed him headed back to our house. Spinning around, I confronted him in our driveway.

"Get out of the car and give me your keys."

He did, and I told him to get in my car. Nick's backpack was slung over his shoulder, but I found another in his car. I looked inside briefly and saw it wasn't books or schoolwork. It looked like drug-related items, but I didn't know and had no experience in this area.

"What are you going to do with it? Give it back to me," Nick demanded with red eyes darting from the backpack to me and back.

"I'm not sure yet."

I threw it in my car and while he pleaded with me to return it.

"I cannot believe you're skipping school and smoking pot. I trusted you, and this is what I get!" I yelled.

When we arrived back several minutes later, he headed toward class, and I found the school resource deputy. With the backpack's contents laid out, I asked if I should be worried. He looked at the scale, a vape, baggies, and some other paraphernalia. He calmly suggested I talk with Nick about the items. I asked him to keep an eye on Nick. The last thing I needed was another troubled kid.

Somehow, I had slipped back into my own faulty reasoning of the past. I naively hoped God wouldn't allow anything to happen with Nick because of the tough road with Katie. And hadn't Paul's drinking and coming out of the closet earned me some sort of extra credit? With a crash back to reality, I realized that Nick was on the wrong path, and I was expecting God to follow my script once again.

Chapter Sixteen

You gain strength, courage, and confidence by every experience in which you stop to look fear in the face. You are able to say to yourself, 'I have lived through this horror and can take the next thing that comes along.'
You must do the thing you think you cannot do.

Eleanor Roosevelt

The traumatic events I'd been through with Katie should have been the most horrible things I would ever experience as a parent, but I was wrong. After years of Katie being in placement, divorcing Paul, and discovering he was gay, I found myself on Mother's Day sitting in the psychiatric unit at the hospital with Nick. His own trauma and pain had been too much to bear, and he thought the solution was downing fistfuls of prescription medication to end his life.

His suicide attempt was, by far, the most horrific thing I'd faced, and it rocked my world … my heart, broken. I had always believed he could overcome whatever troubled him. He had so much potential. Somehow, I thought God would bless Nick because Katie would never be okay.

Nothing could describe my brokenness as I realized that not just one, but both children, were struggling with major depression and anxiety. Nick had all the symptoms—he'd lost interest in surfing and skating, was irritable, sluggish, and not sleeping well. How could I have been so blind? My eternal hope had once again marred my ability to see what was right in front of me. I was still embracing the lie that if I were a wholesome, moral person who followed God, my life would be blessed. And I thought God would protect Nick because Katie was so damaged. My warped thinking was adding to the trauma.

When I was pregnant with Nick, the medical staff said they wouldn't let you labor for over twenty-four hours after your water broke for the mother and baby's safety. After being induced, I psyched myself up, saying that I could do anything for a day. But at twenty-four hours, Nick wasn't quite ready to be born. Since we were both okay, the doctor wanted to keep him in for another ten to twelve hours before taking him out by c-section. I felt a little like I'd done my twenty-four hours of labor with the trauma of my parenting journey, and I couldn't do anymore. Wasn't there a guarantee that God wouldn't give you more than you could handle?

In the months before Nick's suicide attempt, our relationship had deteriorated. He'd said I was a terrible, horrible, no good, very bad mother. Evidently, I had never loved and cared for him. I was selfish and self-centered. I lived in a world of white picket fences and had never gone through anything complicated. He believed I had lived the perfect life. When I had chosen to make the best of things to shield him from the most challenging parts of life, reminding him to trust God, I thought I was doing the right thing. Yet, he believed I was clueless about the realities of life's hardships.

I recalled the first Mother's Day after I miscarried for the first time. At church that Sunday, they asked the mothers to stand. I sat in sadness and willed my heart not to break in public. I excused myself to the restroom, where I tried to contain the tears that leaked out of my eyes. I was a mother. I had just never got to hold the baby that I conceived. Or the next one. By the third time I was pregnant, it was hard to be excited. Getting pregnant three times in one year was hard on the body and the mind, and I knew I couldn't do it again.

Then a precious, healthy, perfect baby boy was born. Nine pounds, two ounces, twenty inches at thirty-seven and a half weeks. It seemed all the difficulties of the pregnancy had earned me an easy baby. He slept through the night at six weeks old. He captivated me with his smile and his curious personality. When Katie came along, he was nearly three. With her big brown eyes, she cautiously observed the world and tried to figure out how she got to this place that was so different from the orphanage.

As Mother's Days passed, I put on a brave face and held my breath for some progress or improvement, believing the next year had to get better. I felt guilty because I should have been grateful for my children, both of whom are miracles. But I grieved for the "mothering" experiences I missed with Katie.

So, on *this* Mother's Day, I sat by my traumatized son's hospital bed, waiting for the drugs to wear off. I wished I could resign from this position of mother, the one I had desperately longed for but now wore like a badge of shame ... the dream of Hallmark moments filled with cards, flowers, and breakfast in bed long vanished. I fiercely believed everything would be okay. But here I was, wishing a simple resignation from motherhood could remove the unbearable pain that was crushing my soul.

Nick's accusations that I was a horrible mother reverberated in my head like a steel drum. I was an epic failure as a parent. My kids needed me in ways I didn't know how to fulfill. Shame filled my tightly wound body, and I feared dissolving into tears at any moment. But even as my utter defeat as a parent absorbed me, my job provided a lifeline.

Two weeks after Nick's overdose, we had an oil spill off our coast, and I worked in the Emergency Operations Center, providing public information. It was a significant incident as hundreds of people from many agencies around the county showed up to work on it. I loved the intensity of the situation, the energy of the work, and the variety of people I met. As a single woman open to dating, my friends called it a target-rich environment due to all the single men working the incident.

After our long days at work, a group of us always went out for a late dinner to decompress. It felt like what I should have done in college. We laughed and shared stories and had a great time. Those six weeks were exhausting, yet so much fun.

After Nick's overdose, another scarlet letter on my parenting, the positive attention from those working the spill was a welcome ego boost. As was my pattern, I distracted myself from the heart-wrenching aspects of my personal life by thrusting myself into the job I knew how to do. I was a horrible mother, but excelled at work.

After the suicide attempt, Nick went to an adolescent psychiatric hospital for a week. It looked like a juvenile hall. Kids sprawled on the gray linoleum floor and broken wooden chairs, playing cards and sassing the staff. Some were asleep, while others verbally prodded each other, trying to elicit a response. Sweat and teenage hormones filled the air as the students waited in line for their medications. They opened their mouths, swallowed, and stuck out their tongues to show they'd taken the pills.

Paul and I each visited several times, but received no guidance or support on how to help Nick. While Nick was safe that week, I feared he would be worse off in the long-term because of the negative lessons from the teenagers who had been there repeatedly. When Nick came home, I made therapy and psychiatry appointments for him. He was fidgety, and anger seeped from his teenage pores. The doctor prescribed benzodiazepines, which just exacerbated his moods. He couldn't sleep and wanted me to rub his back until he finally dozed off. He talked for hours, and his honesty about his feelings was the only benefit of the medication.

Somehow, he passed his junior year, and I furiously looked for something positive to fill summer. I found a program in Minnesota called Outward Bound Intercept. The website said, "Intercept is a program for families with struggling teens and at-risk youth. It helps youth navigate through that treacherous water, teaches them skills to ease the transition, and encourages them to learn more about themselves as a whole human being."

A three-week camping and canoeing expedition followed by community service and a family conference seemed to be a good fit for Nick's nature-loving soul. I asked Paul what he thought because I was at a loss about keeping Nick safe that summer. Paul agreed this could be an outstanding experience for Nick and split the cost with me. Then I talked to Nick about it. While he wasn't thrilled at the prospect of being away from his friends for a month, Nick knew he needed help he couldn't get at home. With less than two weeks before the program's start, I moved quickly to enroll him. When he refused to complete the application, I told him to dictate his answers. One question asked about substance abuse. He paused, not wanting to respond. But my patience had run out.

"Just tell me. It doesn't matter at this point. I just need to fill in the blanks."

He listed drugs I did not know he was using in alarming quantities, which I was sure he understated.

Where had he gotten them? How did he pay for them? When he told me he'd run out of medication and I pleaded for a refill on his behalf, had I unknowingly taken part in drug abuse?

These were yet more questions to which I didn't have answers. But his drug use was a dagger to my heart, something I never imagined would be part of my parenting journey when I read *What to Expect When You're Expecting* Outward Bound accepted him, and I hoped it would be a turning point for both of us.

My mind, though, returned to the familiar question of why God was allowing this? How had I, the good girl, ended up with a drug-abusing son? Hadn't I already been through enough?

My month alone was a little slice of heaven with long-overdue self-care. One evening, I met two girlfriends after work for a lemon drop martini. I loved the sweet and tart combination. As we were sharing stories and laughing, my head throbbed, and my brain was fuzzy. I told them I wasn't feeling well, and they asked when I had eaten last. I said it had been hours.

"You're buzzed!" said one friend.

"What?"

"You're buzzed. Wait. You've never felt this?" the other friend asked

"Ugh. I don't like this feeling. Make it go away," I moaned.

We went to get some food, and I started feeling better.

There were many reasons I didn't drink. My parents never drank, and I always feared the challenges of managing it with my diabetes. Plus, I was constantly dieting and didn't need the extra calories. During my marriage, I needed to be clearheaded because someone needed to be in charge of the children. But over the past year, with Katie in treatment and Nick old enough to drive, I figured I could have one occasionally. It felt exciting to order something other than Diet Coke at a bar. I felt more spunky, flirty, and desirable. After that night, though, I didn't care to drink again

I had been on a lot of dates in the seven months since I'd been online dating. I hadn't met many good guys and had planned to deactivate my account for a while. Dating was exhausting. But then a guy named Tom contacted me. After chatting for a week, he asked me to coffee on a Friday afternoon.

His blue eyes sparkled when I introduced myself. We sat for a long time and shared our stories, hopes, and fears. He was funny, unpretentious, and authentic. We connected on a deep level. Over the following months, Tom and I started dating exclusively. After years of alcohol and drug abuse, he was in recovery and provided me with great insight into parenting Nick.

While Nick was in Minnesota, it was time for emotional self-care, too. I thought the lowest points of my life were over. I should have felt better, but I was still struggling. It was like my pattern in an emergency. I got through it and then melted down. In the same way, I'd lived through years of dark days and was now, on what felt like the "other side" of the trauma, I was experiencing feelings I had never expressed. My inner voice nagged me, asking if I was enough, telling me there was something wrong with me, and second-guessing every decision. That critic had been on overdrive since childhood, and I had built up an emotional fortress that needed to come down. I hated feeling broken, but I'd read that the broken ones were used to help others, so I reluctantly accepted that as my path and scheduled an appointment with a new therapist.

My mind grappled with distressing thoughts. If I had been prettier and thinner, my mom would have loved me more. I would have been more desirable and attractive. More guys would have been interested in me, and maybe I wouldn't have fallen for a gay guy. If I were perfect enough, I wouldn't have had to go through all I did, or I would have managed it better.

When I shared these feelings with the therapist, she asked me to talk more about my childhood and my family's life growing up. What was my mom like? How did my dad act? What was my relationship with my brother? Were there other relatives involved regularly? How did I feel at home?

The memories of my mother's words taunted me. *Don't go out without lipstick. When I was your age, I had lots of dates. You must look good. That seems too tight for you. You're too sensitive. Don't be lazy. Do the right thing. Don't embarrass the family.* She scolded me for sneaking Oreos and being chubby, but

I had to clean my plate because "children in Africa were starving." It didn't matter that I was an outstanding, well-rounded student and a wholesome kid, I always felt like I had to be perfect. I never felt like enough. The messages I received loud and clear were: You don't have it that bad. Stop feeling sorry for yourself. Suck it up, buttercup.

For junior high, my parents enrolled Brian and me in a private Christian school near the college where my dad worked. The transition wasn't as bad as expected and it ended up being an incredible blessing. Afternoons were filled with basketball and volleyball practice, and walks to the popcorn shop on the main street with my new friends. Instead of being teased, my sweet group of friends shoved encouraging notes into each other's lockers.

As an eighth grader, I chose Jeremiah 29:11-13 as my life verse. *"For I know the plans I have for you, declares the Lord. Plans to prosper you and not to harm you. Plans for hope and a future ... if you seek me you will find me if you seek me with all your heart."*

I wholeheartedly believed if I loved God and acted with integrity, I would prosper and not have unpleasant struggles. It provided a script for me to follow. Just as I was preparing my application for a private Christian high school, my parents dropped the bomb that we were moving to California. The thought of starting over again horrified me. I was insecure about my body—both with the diabetes and my weight, and didn't want to be different. My conservative attire and temperament would not fit in with the California I'd heard about. My dark, wavy hair, and fluffy body didn't scream California babe and I didn't speak valley girl.

While my parents longed to return to their roots, the move terrified me. I preferred the safe bubble of Illinois. Somehow, I believed people in California were wild and ridiculous. They spoke diverse languages, voted for Democrats, and weren't God-fearing Christians. I would have to attend a public school with over a thousand students.

On a warm July day, after driving across country in our two cars, we arrived at our new home in a comfortable neighborhood in Goleta, just north of Santa Barbara. The girl across the street and I bonded quickly. We walked around our neighborhood and she gave me the rundown on the local high school with the knowledge she'd learned from her older sister. She and my brother were both in eighth grade.

My parents had picked out a church with a good youth program and I started meeting people there, too. After a month or so, I thought I just might survive the move.

In the fall of my freshman year, someone invited me to a party. I barely recognized anybody and meandered. People were drinking, and it was loud and hot inside, so I went to get fresh air and noticed a girl smoking a cigarette. She asked if I wanted one, and I declined. I had no interest in smoking or drinking because of the potential effect on my diabetes. But above all else, I didn't want to disappoint my parents. They didn't drink or smoke, and I didn't know anyone who did.

Playing on the basketball team and writing for the school newspaper filled my extra time. I worked hard and earned good grades. I was amiable and didn't create trouble. My rebellion was eating McDonald's Big Macs and chocolate shakes after basketball games and not caring about my blood sugar. I lied to my doctor about everything—the results of my urine checks, the amount of insulin I was using, the food I was eating, and how often I exercised. My three-month blood sugar tests told the truth about my lack of control, but I thought it was my little secret, letting myself be imperfect at something that no one other than my doctor saw.

My friends and I talked about boys and intentionally hung around the lockers of those we liked. Occasionally one would ask me out, but it was infrequent. I concentrated on what I was good at and expected I would meet someone as great as my dad, who would find me attractive enough to date, love, and marry.

My dad and I continued to have a solid relationship. I was rarely unhappy with him, except for the day I purchased a mini skirt with my hard-earned babysitting money. It was hardly mini, as it hit just above the knee. But he made me return it because of the message it would send to boys, and I cried at the sales counter, so disappointed.

Meanwhile, I tried to avoid my mom. She was very popular in high school with many guys interested in her. But I wasn't that girl. I felt criticized by her for everything from my looks to my weight to my diabetes control to not being social enough. She seemed more interested in what I was wearing and my social schedule than my grades.

One day I ran down the stairs, and she told me to put on some lipstick

"But I'm going to basketball practice."

"You should put it on anyway."

I rolled my eyes and left.

Her mother, Grammy, told her the same thing. Ironically, Grammy was one of my most supportive family members. I recall sitting on the tall guest bed in her Yorba Linda home when I was thirteen or fourteen. She asked me what I wanted to do with my life and encouraged me to do anything I wanted.

She said, "You're so smart. You could become a Supreme Court Justice because you have such good, moral judgment."

She believed in me, which led me to believe in myself. Throughout the rest of high school, and even college, I thought I could do anything I set my mind to and achieve something meaningful and significant. I intended to make a positive impact on the world.

When I relayed these experiences to the therapist, she asked if I would do a technique known as EMDR (Eye Movement Desensitization and Reprocessing), and I agreed. She explained it was a treatment for trauma and post-traumatic stress disorder. In it, you recall distressing events, and the therapist directs eye movements. I frowned at the thought I had experienced trauma. Trauma was what Katie experienced while starving in the Russian orphanage. Abused and neglected children had trauma. *My family loved me, so I couldn't have trauma, could I?* At that point, I would do anything to relieve my pain.

In the session, no traumatic memory from childhood came to mind, so I recalled one that was irritating but didn't evoke any feelings in my body. I described the exchange with my mother over wearing lipstick. That was all I could remember as a painful experience.

There were many things I wished my mom would have said: "Valerie, honey, I know we are different. You are a smart, talented, beautiful girl with so much to offer. I know you feel less than because of your weight and your diabetes. But it's who you are on the inside that matters. You're so creative and such a gifted writer."

But she never did.

The therapist kept insisting I had trauma, but I just couldn't see it. So, I stopped working with her and began reading and listening to everything I could to develop my emotional intelligence. It shocked me when I realized I never read any non-fiction books not found in a Christian bookstore. The Bible had been my foundation for all life's answers, but I realized there was wisdom in all sorts of writing, so I started asking friends for recommendations and soaked up books and podcasts by Brené Brown, Kristin Neff, Eckhart Tolle, Richard Rohr, and others.

One day I heard a podcast conversation centered on why one woman wanted a wedding ceremony.

She said, "I want that one day to be evidence to the world and myself that I am worthy of being chosen."

Big, ugly tears rolled down my face. I wanted to feel treasured and wanted to know that one other person believed I was more than enough. And I needed everyone else to see that one other person adored me.

As I absorbed this new material, I journaled about the topics that resonated and examined what parts spoke to my wounds. I started a file of letters I could never actually send, but the process helped me express scary feelings without damaging myself or my relationship with others. Working through that muck was brutal, but worth it.

It finally dawned on me I had choices, much like the *Choose Your Own Adventure* novels from my youth. Those books had a variety of endings that were intriguing. It was my moment to choose a different ending to my story. I stopped letting life happen to me and began making choices that served my soul.

Chapter Seventeen

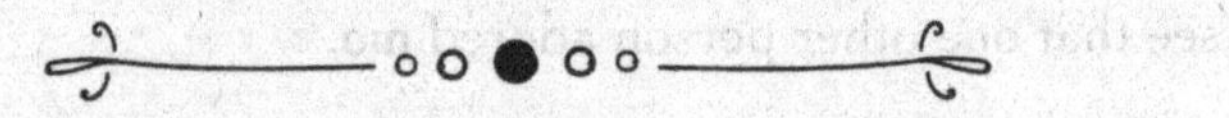

I think midlife is when the universe gently places her hands upon your shoulders, pulls you close, and whispers in your ear: "I'm not screwing around. It's time. All of this pretending and performing—those coping mechanisms that you've developed to protect yourself from feeling inadequate and getting hurt—has to go. Time is growing short. There are unexplored adventures ahead of you. You can't live the rest of your life worried about what other people think. You were both worthy of love and belonging. Courage and daring are coursing through you. You were made to live and love with your whole heart. It's time to show up and be seen.

Brené Brown

When I was younger, I thought only men who wanted younger wives, faster cars, and fuller hairlines experienced midlife crises. People gossiped about them and judged their bad choices. It was plausible that I was having a midlife crisis, but I reframed my thinking. I couldn't have known what I needed at eighteen or twenty-four or even forty because I hardly knew who I was. It was okay to change my mind, and I realized that this was not a midlife crisis but my true adult self emerging. A new awareness stripped away the lies I'd believed and false expectations I'd burdened myself with. I was stepping into who I was meant to be.

My month-long parenting vacation left me refreshed and ready to see Nick again. Paul and I flew to Minnesota to attend the parent retreat. While Nick lived with me full time, Paul wanted to go to support Nick. This interest in being present for his son was a benefit of his newfound sobriety and an amends of sorts.

I couldn't wait to see Nick, but I wondered how he would react to me. While I hadn't missed our daily drama, I was curious about what he was thinking and feeling. We hadn't separated on the best terms.

Two weeks earlier, during the mid-program update, the staff reported Nick excelled in the physical tasks, was conscientious about including others, showing tenacity and natural leadership skills. When Nick shared about his situation and drug use, it helped others open up. He struggled with disorganization and was prone to anger. But overall, he was becoming more self-aware and mastering the skills required to exist in the wilderness.

The first part of the retreat was just for the parents. We learned our students had been working on some communication and boundary-setting strategies. It differed from any of Katie's parenting workshops. These kids had enormous potential but were temporarily off track. I sat with other parents at dinner, discussing our hopes that our kids had benefited from the program and our relationships would improve.

After dinner that first evening, the staff gave me a letter written by Nick during his "solo" experience toward the end of the trip. During each expedition, every participant spends two to three days in a secluded spot to reflect alone on their journey, with all the food, skills, and supplies they need. One assignment during that experience was to write a letter to their parents. Nick's letter said:

> "Mom, I'm sorry that my behavior had become so careless and disrespectful that you had to send me away. I appreciate you sent me to a place that would constructively help me rather than punish me for my mistakes. I appreciate that you're so caring to everyone and humble about your achievements, even if you're not going to make a single penny. You always put other people's needs above your own. I think you're one of the strongest people I know, given all you've been through. You always keep a smile on your face even though you're pushing through new struggles every day. I think one thing we could work on collectively is communication with one another. Often I feel like we are not on the same page. One strength that I have is the ability to hold in strong emotions. The problem is that I let

them build up until I burst. I would like you to talk to me more maturely rather than treating me like a little kid. I'm willing to compromise many things according to what it will take. Even if it means losing freedom or everything that I have because I think my reckless behavior ruined our relationship, I hope we can regain trust and respect for each other. Love, Nick

P.S. I wrote this on a log in the woods, so sorry for the sloppy writing.

As I read through it, I felt encouraged and hopeful and couldn't wait to see him.

The next day, Paul and I stood outside with the other parents, anxiously awaiting our students. Each family group seemed to have a similar tentative reunion on the grassy area outside the meeting hall. But as soon as the students started teaching us about their wilderness experience, the awkwardness passed. The students showed us their seventy-pound packs, demonstrated how they portaged canoes on their shoulders, and how they set up their tents. Nick carried his seventy-five-pound boat for a mile in the final thirteen-mile personal challenge event, including canoeing, portaging, and running. It impressed me. Not only did he carry it, but he and his closest teammate also beat the rest of the group by over twenty minutes. I could see the work he'd put in through the muscle definition in his arms, his chiseled cheekbones, and how his pants hung loosely on his body.

At another session, the students showed a map of Minnesota's Outer Boundary Waters map, a labyrinth of lakes near the Canadian border. The team described their 178-mile canoe and hiking journey, the daily schedule, and how they learned to work together, planning their routes, assigning chores, and supporting each other through challenging tasks. In their presentation, we saw photos of their gritty faces streaked with mud and sweat, the beautiful wilderness, and their teamwork in action. They spoke about rock climbing, their high-rope course, and their three-day solo experience. The journey had changed them. It was encouraging to see their affection and gratitude for each other and their leaders.

Afterward, Paul and I met with Nick and his leader to discuss our family's challenges and plan how to move forward. I apologized for focusing so much on Katie's crises, and Paul shared he was sorry he missed so much of Nick's life because of his drinking. Nick acknowledged how his drug use led to angry outbursts and disrespectful behaviors. We worked on communication strategies, and Nick listed his one-week, one-month, and one-year goals, focusing on not relapsing, finishing school, and rebuilding relationships. It was a productive conversation, and we headed home after his graduation ceremony. I felt optimistic our life together would improve.

Nick immediately started his senior year when we returned home, and I put our house on the market. The house I lived in, which I'd shared with various people over the previous four years, was my dream house in my ideal neighborhood. I loved everything about it—the layout, the beautiful orchard view, and the tree-lined street. I loved my neighbors and my two-mile commute to work. Nick hated leaving behind the man cave where he and his friends hung out and probably took a lot of drugs. But I thought a reset might help solidify the changes he set out to make after his Outward Bound experience. Moving from that home marked the end of the dream for the happy family of four. There was a grief I couldn't describe, despite knowing our lives were better.

My house sold in ten days, but finding a replacement was challenging because of the housing market. I knew God had a place for me. I just needed to find it and eventually moved from my big family home on Camino Venturoso, the street of adventure, to a three-bedroom home on Calle Esperanza, the street of hope.

The new house needed some work, and I was excited to make it my own. Paint colors like *white picket fence, burlap,* and *clean slate* went on my walls, appropriate in both hue and sentiment. Dad and I worked on various projects, from painting to tiling to turning a dresser into a bathroom vanity, and I loved our time together. It reminded me of the days as a young girl when I would hang out with him in the garage listening to the Dodgers' game on the radio while he worked on our cars. Most of all, I enjoyed having a new focus and creating a space to comfort and inspire my soul. The project was yet another layer of my self-discovery.

As the weeks passed, Nick attempted school and a part-time job as a valet, but things weren't clicking. He hadn't been able to transfer the high of his summer experience into his daily life. He became irritable, so I spoke with his psychiatrist about changing medications. But I never knew if extracurricular drugs were involved. I hated confronting Nick because it never ended well, and I hadn't mastered the communication skills learned at the parenting conference. Contracts and natural consequences didn't seem to work, and I didn't have any other tools in my parenting repertoire.

By November, every day with Nick was unpredictable. It was bad or worse, but rarely even keeled. I wondered if he would punch a hole in the wall or yell at me. Every time I received a text alert about a car accident, I wondered if Nick was the driver responsible for it with his reckless behavior and self-medication. His behavior was increasingly unsafe, and I couldn't tolerate his actions for much longer. Nick's eighteenth birthday was roaring toward me like a freight train. He would be an "adult," and I would no longer be legally responsible for him on January eighth. But I had no idea on how to help him move forward in a good direction. I wished we could go back to the Outward Bound for a refresher.

On Thanksgiving, Tom, with whom I was now in a committed relationship, celebrated with his family while Nick stayed home to surf. When I returned, Nick told me he tried to hang himself from the top of our staircase. While I was distraught, those statements no longer shocked me. I had experienced too many variations on that theme.

Nick was out of control—and fear paralyzed me. It threw me back into the chaos of my life with Paul and Katie. In those days, our family was like a balance board. Nick and I counterbalanced Paul's and Katie's moods. But now, it was just Nick and me, and we were seriously off balance.

A bright contrast to my situation with Nick was my relationship with Tom. He was everything my forty-something self needed, and my twenty-four-year-old self never knew she wanted. He was funny and insightful, gentle, and yet very masculine. We loved watching sports, going to the beach, and soaking in the serenity of the mountains. He enjoyed learning about everything from astronomy to home repair to disc golf and didn't seem intimidated by things he didn't know. His purpose in life was to pass on the gift of sobriety he'd received, and I admired his passion for helping others, something that was also important to me.

At his suggestion, I tried Al-Anon to manage my emotions surrounding Nick. Since I didn't know what to expect, I convinced a friend to go with me to the first meeting in a dark room in an unfamiliar church. I was uncharacteristically nervous about walking into a group of strangers. A circle of despondent individuals read a passage from a twelve-step recovery book and then shared on the topic. It was so discouraging as person after person talked about their decades-old family wounds. I saw nothing I wanted there. But I was shocked at the realization my children might need help because I didn't protect them from the effects of alcoholism in our family. The following week I went to a beginners' meeting for those unfamiliar with the program, thinking it might be better. But it was not helpful, either. Even though I knew I should try again, I didn't.

Another friend invited me to a newly formed support group for moms of struggling teenagers, and I was desperate enough to try it. Usually, no one could relate to my situation with Katie, and I just felt frustrated. But this one was different because the conversation could be about whichever child of mine was causing me heartache that day. Being together with six to eight women each Tuesday was a welcome relief. We sat with two facilitators and poured our hearts out, describing the highs and lows of the previous week. We spoke of the heartaches too devastating to share with other parents in our circles. It was the first time I felt understanding and support from another parent walking through similarly rough circumstances. Although the students in the group struggled with different things, it was a relief to open up about my challenges, and I wished I had found the group earlier. An authentic life was so much richer than the life I lived for so many years.

Chapter Eighteen

If you focus on the hurt, you will continue to suffer.
If you focus on the lesson, you will continue to grow.

Unknown

I thought a trip to visit my brother's family in Colorado for Christmas might be fun … a refresh for Nick and me. Nick seemed cautiously excited but was concerned about what his young cousins would think of him. I told him they knew nothing about his struggles. All they cared about was playing with him.

The flight from Santa Barbara to Los Angeles was fine, but Nick's anxiety ramped up while we were waiting at the airport. I thought eating might help, but his knee bounced as he fidgeted, so we left the restaurant. Moments later, Nick freaked out and threw his phone, shattering the glass, which just angered him more. As he walked away, I feared I would lose him amid the thousands of holiday travelers. I handed him my iPad, hoping he wouldn't throw it, too, so we could have some way of communicating. Frantic, I called my parents, who were already in Colorado, to give them an update. Then I called Paul to ask if he would pick Nick up from the airport and keep him for a few days. He said no because he also had Christmas plans. So I hung up and paced the airport walkways for what seemed like hours, praying for some solution.

Nick showed up at the gate on time, and I exhaled as we boarded the plane. I gave him some anti-anxiety medication to settle him down. But by the time we landed in Denver, his anxiety had increased, and by two a.m., he was yelling and jumped out of our rental car. I prayed he wasn't hurt and pleaded with him to get back in. After a few minutes, he did, and we were both exhausted. When we arrived at Brian's house, I wondered if I had made a colossal mistake.

Nick's struggles were another secret I kept for several reasons. First, it was his story to tell. Second, our family was already so messed up, no one would believe me, mainly because people thought we exaggerated Katie's issues. But with Nick, he had his entire life ahead of him, full of promise. Finally, I didn't want to share anything that might somehow impact his future or bring unnecessary judgment on him or me.

Thankfully, when the cousins—aged two, six, eight, ten, and twelve—woke up the following day, they did not know what had transpired through the night, even though all the adults had deep creases under their eyes. The kids loved having their big buddy around to skateboard, snowboard, and joke around with. Around the cousins, Nick kept it together. But at night, he was restless and irritable, struggling to sleep and manage his emotions.

On Christmas morning, trying to make the best of things, I wrote a social media post:

> All is calm, yet all is bright as I look at the giant Christmas tree. Soon the pitter-patter of my nieces' and nephews' little feet will scamper to grab their stockings. It's cold outside in Colorado with snow on the ground. But once again, we are missing Katie. It's our third Christmas apart, and while this is our new normal, it doesn't feel as it should be. She'll be celebrating with the other girls on her team and her favorite staff. Yesterday they made Christmas cookies, and today she'll get to open the presents we sent. We talked to her last night, and she sounded terrific. While she's missing being here with her brother, grandparents, aunt and uncle, and cousins, she knows that it's just not in the plan right now. I read an article about why we ask "Why me?" When something terrible happens, but we don't ask the same thing when blessed. In that spirit, I acknowledge my joy in seeing my nephew with leukemia ski for an entire day. I thank God my mom's kidney cancer is in remission. My heart is full of love for those

> who walked through life with me and filled my soul. I am truly blessed. And while I miss Katie and grieve the life I thought I would have, I look forward to a new year.

At least I was honest at the end … grieving the life I thought I would have. The rest of it was just my eternally hopeful soul trying to be optimistic.

We made it back to Santa Barbara without incident, but I felt overwhelmed, unsure what to do next.

In January, Nick had a severe psychotic episode. Whatever he took caused him to lose his sight temporarily, and he started freaking out. The friend he was hanging out with drove him to the psychiatrist's office. Nick's doctor called to tell me what was happening and said Nick needed inpatient treatment. Our approach wasn't working, and it relieved me to have someone else offering guidance. I called Paul and asked him to figure out what treatment options were available through his insurance. He did the research and got approval for Nick to detox at our local hospital. Nick agreed to go, but asked to delay a day to see his friends before checking in. I allowed that because I was so grateful he agreed to go, and I believed he'd follow through.

The day he was to check into the program, Tom and I headed out of town so he could introduce me to his son, Adam. I wrestled with whether to cancel my plans and decided that the only benefit of staying at home was to make sure Nick got to the hospital. *But honestly, would it have mattered?* I couldn't force him into a vehicle if he didn't want to go, and my only other option would be to kick him out of my house. I asked Paul for help in making sure Nick got checked in and jotted Nick a note saying I loved him and was proud that he was taking action to get healthy. Praying fervently, I tried to let go.

Nick followed through on the plan, going into the hospital to detox just two weeks after his eighteenth birthday. I felt relieved he had done what he said he would. When I contacted him a few days later, his general anger surprised me. I didn't know about the physical effects of detoxing and wasn't prepared for him to be pissed off. I naively thought things would be better. From the hospital, he went to a twenty-eight-day inpatient rehab facility. When I visited, he stood behind the kitchen, smoking cigarettes, as if to say, you can't tell me what to do, mom. He didn't acknowledge my presence. At that moment, I didn't think Nick could like me any less.

How did I become the bad guy? Wasn't I the responsible parent, the one always there for him, ready to take him surfing, making him and his friends food at all hours, and helping him out with money when he needed it? Why was God allowing this to happen?

I was desperate to get out of my pain, so I started attending family support groups and Al-Anon I'd dismissed. I saw how recovery had saved Tom, and I wanted what he had. Like with most things, once I made a decision, I was all in. I went to several meetings each week, volunteered, asked a woman to sponsor me, and worked the twelve steps.

Nick got clean, but it was rough as we navigated the new experience of mother and adult son. Learning to set boundaries was hard. We agreed that he'd stay in a sober living house for a month after completing the rehab program. But he didn't enjoy living with washed-up middle-aged men and left without talking to me. He thought I'd let him stay at my house. But I told him that wouldn't work for me because it wasn't what we'd agreed upon. My mothering side wanted to solve his problem, but the woman I was becoming in recovery knew I needed to set and keep boundaries.

Early the following day, I took my dog out for her walk. Nick's car sat in the visitor spot in my homeowner's association parking, his long, lean frame curled up in the front seat. It broke my heart to know he had a head cold and sore throat. I cried as I walked. It was one of the hardest things I've ever done. But I knew I had finally done the right thing for myself and for Nick.

I got used to being okay with not knowing where he was or if he was safe. His choices were out of my control. Nick moved around, living with friends, and then my parents, and then back with me. I was clear about my expectations and consequences and stopped handling things for him. While I wanted him to stay clean, I wanted my house to be the peaceful retreat I'd created.

He started working and surfing more and found different friends. When he couldn't stand his dull valet job any longer, he asked for my help. I encouraged him to go back to working construction. From a young age, Nick was interested in tools and building. He loved working alongside my dad. They had constructed a treehouse, half-pipe, and other assorted projects over the years. Everything Nick knew about building had come from my dad and his own trial and error. The summer before his junior year, Nick worked for our neighbor who owned a construction company. Nick was a hard worker who had sometimes been unreliable because of his drug use. But he had talent. So, Nick and I strategized about approaching his former boss about a job. It was a challenge for a kid with social anxiety to advocate for himself. But Nick arranged a meeting and was honest about how he'd changed his life. He was offered a full-time position, which became a turning point in Nick's young adult life. I cried with gratitude.

Chapter Nineteen

There are no negative emotions.
There are just unskillful ways for
coping with the emotions that we can't bear.

Suzanne Stabile

It was the end of February, and discouragement overwhelmed me while scrolling through social media. I needed to remember posts were a tiny slice of curated reality, but I still felt disappointed in the experiences I'd missed out on, like the college application process with Nick, and shopping for a homecoming dress with Katie. While I hadn't had those experiences, I appreciated those I had. I heard a million conversations, logging hundreds of miles, taking the boys to surf. I'd served bacon and pancakes for Nick's friends at my house every Thursday morning of junior high. The year Katie did Girl Scouts, I stood outside the grocery store with her as she sold cookies. My kids progressed in a thousand ways, unseen in a classroom, athletic field, or reflected in social media posts.

Still, it was hard as I grieved the loss of so many dreams. Katie never enjoyed the toys of my childhood and never wanted a dollhouse like mine. She didn't play with dolls, hated shopping, and never read books. We didn't have any common interests, and our relationship was based solely on practical matters—like eating, visiting the doctor, and going to school.

But there were some signs of progress. Katie had been in Utah for one year and appeared more emotionally level and healthy when I visited for a parent workshop and treatment team meeting. Parenting a special needs child was lonely, and I enjoyed the interaction with the other parents who came for the workshop. Somehow, I ended up in a group with parents of substance-abusing students. One family shared their daughter's college acceptance. It was encouraging to hear her story of transformation, given Nick's recent experience. But as I sat there, I wanted to scream. For these families, it was realistic that their kids could recover and thrive.

Each time I attended a workshop, I was looking for some seed of hope that Katie could have a stable and independent future. Each time I was disappointed. I knew I should not have unrealistic expectations or hope, but Katie could not, and would not, recover. She didn't have a cold or an addiction. She would never be free of autism, reactive attachment disorder, or her early trauma. Thriving was very different in her situation. Perhaps one day, she wouldn't need to carry around her worn stuffed animal named "Steve" and fixate on pillows, saying "pell-o" in her unique style, over and over. Maybe one day, she would speak more clearly so people could understand what she was saying. And I would love to one day share a hotel room with her and not have to listen to her rustling around and making strange sounds for ninety minutes while her body calmed down before falling asleep. I just couldn't picture what her future entailed.

At one of the workshop sessions, the presenter discussed regular self-care—vacations, therapy, exercise, connecting with friends—all of which I did. But I felt like I was on a hamster wheel. I'd think I'd healed from some aspect of life, and then I'd visit Katie, or meet with the school district, or get an incident report and feel the wound was reopened. I wasn't sure if I would ever recover and hated feeling broken.

At home, I continued with therapy and working the twelve steps in Al-Anon. I vowed to use my brokenness to help myself and others and willed myself to deal with all challenging emotions, including my resentments.

Foremost, I resented God. I had lived a moral, ethical life, and my life didn't turn out the way I thought I deserved. What could I have done differently to earn His love and grace and a peaceful life? If He was simply teaching me something, either I was a slow learner, or He was extraordinarily cruel.

I resented myself for not acknowledging Paul's drinking problem earlier, and for blinding myself to my suspicions about his sexuality. I resented Paul for loving alcohol more than he loved the kids and me and for not being honest with himself about his sexuality, too.

I resented Katie's birth mother for drinking and using. Her selfishness set Katie up for a tremendously hard life, which I felt responsible for fixing. I resented my frustration and the effort that, no matter how hard I tried, couldn't heal Katie. I resented my daughter's conditions that had consumed my life since her adoption and the stress, pain, and despair that ensued.

Katie was not the kid I expected, hoped for, or felt equipped to parent. She and I didn't have wonderful mother-daughter experiences, and I couldn't get over it. I wished I was more compassionate and understanding toward her, but exhaustion and trauma and pain had drained me of both. We had adopted Katie with the best of intentions, saving her from a dark, dreary orphanage where she would have died at a young age. The life we had given her, while not optimal, was better than dying in a Russian orphanage. But it seemed completely unfair.

It pained me that I did to Nick what Paul's mom had done to him. I wanted to be his friend more than I wanted to be his mom. I needed an ally in the family disease of alcoholism, and I wrongly put that on him.

And I resented God for not giving me a typical mothering experience with Nick. I thought I had earned a high-achieving student-athlete after dealing with Katie and Paul. I wanted Nick to be like me—a rule-following over-achiever. When his choices caused me so much stress and heartache, I felt angry. It was hard to acknowledge that despite my hopes, and perhaps even my unreasonable needs, Nick was just a very typical high schooler who did what most students in distress do—he looked for the easiest way through the pain.

I resented myself for not seeing what I didn't want to see. I ignored my gut on so many occasions and didn't acknowledge problems until they were so obvious, I could no longer ignore them. I wished I had more self-compassion and love when I was younger and single. Why hadn't I gotten help earlier? Had my desire for perfection and fear of being exposed as *less than* hurt my loved ones and me?

My friend once said, "Back in the day, you looked pretty perfect walking into the office with your green corduroy jacket, cute skirt, and high-heeled boots. You held everything so tight. And your life looked so together."

Appearances can be so misleading.

I came to understand my childlike faith gave me a false picture and very simplistic view of God. I thought that A + B = C and eventually understood, as a more mature adult, God never promised that. There was no formula for a pain-free and easy life. Yet I knew and trusted there was a God and felt better after working through my anger at Him for allowing my family to go through some horrible experiences.

Plus, I needed some hope to hold on to as this never-ending journey continued. I also had to forgive myself and others, shedding the resentments. Holding on to those feelings wasn't helping me. That series of letters I wrote … the ones I could never send … helped to get all my negative emotions onto the page and out of my mind. Once they were written, I found freedom. Sometimes it came quickly, and sometimes it took months. But it came, and I found freedom in releasing those thoughts.

Easter was early that year, and with it came contemplation and reflection on past Easter seasons. I thought about Good Friday and a sermon I'd heard on pain and suffering. The pastor spoke of the significance of the Saturday between Good Friday and Easter Sunday. Good Friday, the day they crucified Jesus, was heartbreaking for his followers. On Saturday, they felt hopeless as He suffered a brutal death on the cross. They couldn't know the joy that resurrection Sunday would bring.

I had many Saturdays in the last three years and hoped to never relive those dark days. Yet, I was thankful for the hard times that had refined me. They had freed me to see the world with a fresh perspective and to live authentically. I saw the blessings in the messes, and my mantra became: I will look forward. I will trust God. Today is a new day.

A few months later, I visited Katie, and while reflecting on her, wrote this poem.

In the moments between the smiles

She retreats

Her face buried in the game with the headphones in the ears

Running from the world.

In the moments between the smiles

There is anxiety and pain

Uncertainty about what to do or how to act

Closed to the world around

In the moments between the smiles

She escapes to a quiet, safe place

One that is more reliable and certain

To her damaged brain.

In the moments between the smiles

I wonder if she thinks about others

Questions reality

And thinks outside the cocoon

Which she has carefully constructed

In the moments between the smiles

Is there life beyond the blank gaze and the vacant eyes?

The fragile emotions and the tender heart?

I wish I could know what it is like for her

In the moments between the smiles.

Katie was a senior in high school, and I finally saw some positive interaction with peers. She no longer isolated herself as much and could exchange a few sentences of everyday conversation. When we visited Barbie, the beautiful dark brown horse she rode, the staff raved about her hard work in the stable. Katie had become a skilled rider and loved working around the stable.

Her emotions were still erratic, though, that bothered me less than it had in previous years. Maybe I'd changed and accepted her emotions, no matter how illogical they were. Instead of wanting her to stop the nonsense, I allowed her to have her feelings, even though it was uncomfortable for me. Her staff continued to work with her mood swings, and I kept hoping for a medication combination that would smooth her moods. She prepared to finish high school and recognized Utah as the best place for her to do that.

Christmas that year was delightful, a welcome contrast to the earlier years. Katie flew home on her own with no issues along the way. I was happy I did not have to make the trip, which sometimes meant flying to Utah and back in one day

We worked on her post-high school plan by meeting with the regional center, which would provide services, and visiting the local community college. She was excited about the path ahead and looked forward to taking swimming, drawing, and songwriting classes in the fall.

We prepared for her to meet Tom's family at Christmas, which was the subject of multiple family therapy calls over the month. The reactive attachment disorder side of Katie would love new people to charm. The autistic side could be easily overwhelmed, and we talked through her coping mechanisms with her therapist.

On Christmas Eve, Tom, Katie, and I arrived early. It was quiet as Katie eased into the house. Sadie, their small dog, bounded into the room, and they became fast friends as Katie sat in front of the fireplace, petting her. As the family gathered, Katie did well and acted appropriately. A few times, when she felt overwhelmed, she sat in the guest room to collect herself. Katie had a blast. At the end of the evening, she told Tom she loved his family. Then announced, "I am definitely coming to Easter."

Chapter Twenty

You can only control what's in your hula hoop.

Unknown

Katie had been away for four years. It had been an enormous measure of grace I didn't see the challenges we'd experience over that time. I don't know how I would have survived if I'd known. I often wondered if Katie would live long enough to graduate high school, given her suicidal thoughts and attempts, and the continual parade of new diagnoses. So, seeing her so close to graduation was a miracle.

Paul, Katie, and I continued to work on her transition back home. It relieved me Paul was taking over Katie's case management, coordinating her medications, therapy appointments, and school. I was ready for a break. In Al-Anon, I learned I no longer needed to be in control of everything.

As graduation day neared, Katie's anxiety soared with the anticipation of returning to a home life that differed completely from what she left. She didn't have any friendships to rekindle, and she would be in college, all while living in a new home in a different part of Santa Barbara. Paul would be her primary caregiver for the first time, and she would live with him and his partner.

I flew to Utah for her graduation and met Paul and his partner, and my parents, for the ceremony. It was a fantastic testament to Katie's accomplishments. She beamed as she chatted with everyone and teared up as she hugged the people, students, and staff who had supported her during the previous two and a half years. The fact she cared about others showed progress. She never had friends at any of the other schools. Katie was more independent, accepted feedback, and changed her actions to the extent she could. She was still an emotional rollercoaster, but her moods were more appropriate and less volatile. She no longer laughed when someone got injured, and she didn't get hurt when someone had a neutral face instead of a smile.

I saw progress in myself, as well. Life was more peaceful because I had a better handle on my thoughts. I accepted who Katie was instead of wishing she was someone she could never be. It helped that I wasn't moving from crisis to crisis, even though challenging events still occurred. Life didn't feel like such a tornado and it took time to stop bracing for Katie-related chaos. Once again, I had to trust God would take care of her. And me.

Several months later, Tom went to my parents' house to ask for their blessing to marry me and proposed on Valentine's Day. We planned an intimate wedding for September and it felt like all the shattered pieces were falling into place. It was a blessed reprieve from the turmoil of the previous five years.

When planning my first wedding, getting every detail exactly right was the priority, as if the perfect wedding would lead to the ideal marriage. My Martha Stewart blue wedding planner went with me everywhere to track everything. My family and I still laugh at a picture of me at my first wedding rehearsal, standing at the front of the church, planner in hand, directing everything like a conductor. I had everything under control.

Twenty-four years later, I was still highly organized, but approached the planning with ease and inquiry. Instead of struggling to fit square pegs in round holes, as had been my recurring practice, I was as flexible and easy-going as a recovering perfectionist could be. If something didn't work out, it wasn't meant to be, and it wasn't personal.

It was amazing to experience life this way and to observe things as they came together, like how I found my wedding dress. One Saturday, Tom went to his twelve-step recovery meeting at the local community center. I planned to do chores around the house and meet up with him afterwards. A few minutes after he left, he texted me a cryptic note about a wedding dress sale taking place. The image didn't come through but, through a quick Google search, I discovered a local non-profit was selling brand new dresses that day. I called my best friend and my mom and they met me at the sale fifteen minutes later. In the worn-down auditorium of a 100-year-old school with makeshift changing stalls and mirrors propped up, I found my dress and felt like a princess in the simple strapless taffeta a-line gown. I glowed as the volunteers fawned over me and floated out the door, excited and marveling at the serendipity.

Tom and I appreciated a successful relationship was built on our commitment to each other, and not the party favors, bridesmaid's dresses, or centerpieces. We recognized how we prioritized our individual and collective emotional, mental, spiritual, and physical health would determine the quality of our marriage. We looked forward to the wedding as the continuation, and not the destination, of our adventure together.

Plans were falling into place. All was well until Tom's dad had a seizure in April. The doctor diagnosed him with glioblastoma, the deadliest form of brain cancer, and said patients in his condition typically had twelve to eighteen months to live. Tom's dad, also named Tom, had been healthy, and the news stunned us. His condition deteriorated more swiftly than predicted, and it seemed unlikely he would make it to our wedding. It was terrible to watch him fade away.

But as Tom and I spoke about death, it enhanced our emotional intimacy. We leaned on each other and explored hospice resources, like Frank Ostaseski's *The Five Invitations: Discovering What Death Can Teach Us About Living Fully.*

Our deep discussions focused not merely on what this meant for Tom and his dad, but about how we aspired to be intentional. Growing with my partner in this way was new, and I cherished our profound connection. Like with many of our experiences, it affirmed our desire to have meaningful and authentic lives. We wanted to know when our earthly lives ended; we had lived well.

The tools I learned in Al-Anon helped in so many areas. One of my favorite sayings is "You can only control what's in your hula hoop." I had practiced it many times with Tom and my children, but now got to use it as we navigated challenging family situations. Most situations did not directly involve me, and I had to step back and wait to be asked for input. It took considerable self-control, but it strengthened my emotional muscles each time I did.

Chapter Twenty-One

Joy and sorrow are analogous to the ebb and flow of the ocean tide. They are natural rhythms. And we are mellowed by their presence when we accept them as necessary to our very existence. Any pain today guarantees an equal amount of pleasure, if I willingly accept them both.

Karen Casey, *Each Day a New Beginning*

A few months later, Paul called on a Saturday morning to say he'd found Katie shivering, naked and catatonic on her bed. He got her clothed and took her to the emergency room. I raced to meet them. When I arrived, Paul explained Katie felt sick the previous evening, and he'd given her cold medicine. He guessed she had taken something else in the middle of the night. When the doctor came in to talk to us, Paul shared what happened. The doctor listened and responded that Katie had too much serotonin in her system just to be cold medicine. He asked what else she could have taken. I looked at

Paul as he rattled off the medications at their house. The doctor hinted at an intentional overdose and said Katie's condition was life-threatening. He immediately moved Katie to the intensive care unit to be intubated, and we waited to learn if she would live.

When she woke up twenty-four hours later, my parents, Tom, Nick, Paul, and I talked in her room in the intensive care unit. A nurse pulled me outside to say Katie had been talking about trauma. I wasn't sure what she was referring to since Katie's entire life was traumatic. But most recently, when she was in treatment, a peer had molested her, and there had to be lasting effects from that situation.

But I also didn't trust Katie's definition of trauma and abuse. She had learned many terms from her peers in treatment that garnered attention, and she threw them around just to see how people would react. It reminded me of junior high when she claimed I was abusing her after asking her to do simple chores. Nick's best friend was with us, and he knew I wasn't harming Katie. But I told her I could go to jail with her misstatements if she ever used those terms around others.

As the nurse and I talked outside the room, Katie spoke to the others about her dad's partner being emotionally abusive. My parents walked out, shaking their heads. A few minutes later, Paul strode away to discuss the allegations with his partner, and it was the last time Katie saw him for the next ten months.

Katie then described a horrible scene to Tom and Nick and explained why she tried to kill herself. About ten days earlier, two peers she met at an LGBTQ youth group, a girl and a male transitioning to a female, invited her to a sleepover. Katie enjoyed meeting friendly, accepting people there, and identified as one of those letters, but which one depended on her mood that day. After her dad dropped her off, Katie and her friends started drinking, kissing, and fooling around. Her head hurt, and she was uncomfortable, and said her brain was foggy. They put a dog collar on her and made her crawl naked around the room. They whipped her with the leash, and she sobbed and screamed. She wasn't able to make sense of how to make it stop. They eventually removed the collar, and they all fell asleep. When Paul picked Katie up the next day, she said nothing.

While she described this situation to Tom and Nick, I was still outside talking with the nurse. They didn't want to stop Katie's description of the events, so the guard came out of the room and said I needed to hear the conversation because Katie was talking about sexual assault. The nurse asked me what to do.

"Don't you have protocols for this ... it seems like you should call the Rape Crisis Center and the police," I replied, sighing.

Nick pressed Katie for the address of the apartment where it happened. He was ready to take matters into his own hands. While I was proud he wanted to stand up for her, I cautioned him not to do anything stupid because there was undoubtedly more to the story.

I walked to a quiet corridor to process it all with clenched fists. *How could Katie have been taken advantage of again?* My thoughts shifted quickly. *Is it true?*

Katie was an unreliable source of information, but I knew there must be some element of truth. Katie couldn't invent such a dramatic story. I had to listen to her account, even if it was untrue, exaggerated, or inflated. Whatever happened made her want to die, and I questioned Paul's judgment. *How could he let Katie go to a sleepover with strangers? Did he ever read her texts?* She was so fragile and immature, more like a twelve-year-old.

Rubbing my temples, I walked back to the room to look at Katie's texts and learned she willingly took part in the flirting and drinking. But I doubt she knew the impact her enthusiastic responses would have. *How would I unravel the multidimensional elements of Katie's story and did it really matter?*

Paul wanted to explain his part of the story to me, and I had to distance myself to focus on being Katie's parent. I tried not to assign blame because every tale had two sides. The allegations of emotional abuse by his partner just didn't ring true to who I knew him to be. I suspected Paul's temper triggered Katie, but she couldn't be mad at her dad, so she blamed it on his partner.

That day was a tragic bonding experience for Tom and my kids—Katie as the victim, Nick as the protective big brother, and Tom as a safe and trusted adult who loved them both. Since Katie and Tom's first meeting, she had grown to love him. They had both wished they weren't alive at one point, and she felt connected to him because of it. She'd hug him and say, "Tom and me, we're survivors. We've been through tough stuff, but we made it."

After ten traumatic days in the hospital, Katie moved to a psychiatric hospital for a weekend stay, which never helped her but provided a safe place for her in the interim. My parents offered to have Katie at their house for a while, and I was once again grateful for their commitment to my children. It was unbelievable Katie, just eighteen, had experienced another trauma.

Between Katie's situation, Tom's dad's brain cancer, and wedding planning, we were juggling heavy emotional circumstances. At forty-eight, I finally understood life had a rhythm with highs and lows, and an ebb and flow. As a younger person, I believed life was supposed to be even keeled or euphoric, and if it wasn't, it was your fault. I didn't know many people who had encountered the trials I had, like getting diagnosed with diabetes and kidney disease, so I assumed something was wrong with me. But now, I understood life is not linear. Bad things happened to good people, and good things happened to bad people. Acceptance was the means to contentment and joy, and I felt fortunate I finally learned this lesson. It made the challenges more tolerable, as I no longer blamed myself for everything that went wrong.

Tom and I needed some time away and headed to the Eastern Sierras, one of our favorite spots, to work on our wedding. God's presence was tangible in the mountains, with the crisp air, rippling creeks, and melodic sounds of birds. We tossed around ideas for our ceremony and the prayer our friend and officiant for the day would read. We spent hours side-by-side individually crafting our vows because we wanted every component to reflect love, joy, and the intention we had for our married life.

As people started coming into town for the big event, the complicated parts of our life seemed to pause, and it was a blessed reprieve. The week leading up to it was full of activities with my brother and his family after years of not being together. The last time had been the arduous trip Nick and I took to Colorado at Christmas. It was a joy to see him teaching the younger cousins to surf and for all of them to see Katie for the first time in years.

Our wedding was in a lovely garden at a historic Goleta ranch that had long been a favorite place. Miraculously, Tom's dad made it. His condition had been deteriorating rapidly as the brain cancer took over. He and his caregiver arrived early, and I slipped outside for a quick visit before anyone else came. Taking his hand, I hugged him, hoping the tears in my eyes wouldn't ruin my makeup. His mumbling was incomprehensible, but I knew he was saying, "I love you." It was a precious moment on a magical day.

With the sun shining through the oak trees, an acoustic guitar playing in the background, Tom stood with his son, Adam, by his side. This was yet another miracle. When I met Tom, their bond was just blossoming. Tom's sobriety allowed him to consistently be present in Adam's life. I got to witness the journey of a man learning to be a father to his then eleven-year-old son. And now he was the best man in our wedding, a truly wonderful gift.

Katie walked in as a junior bridesmaid, and Tom's niece, Bella, served as our flower girl. Tom rocked nervously as he waited for me to stand by his side. Tears glistened in his eyes as Nick walked me down the grassy path. It felt intimate as we said our vows in front of forty-five of our closest family and friends.

Tom choked back tears as he spoke his vows.

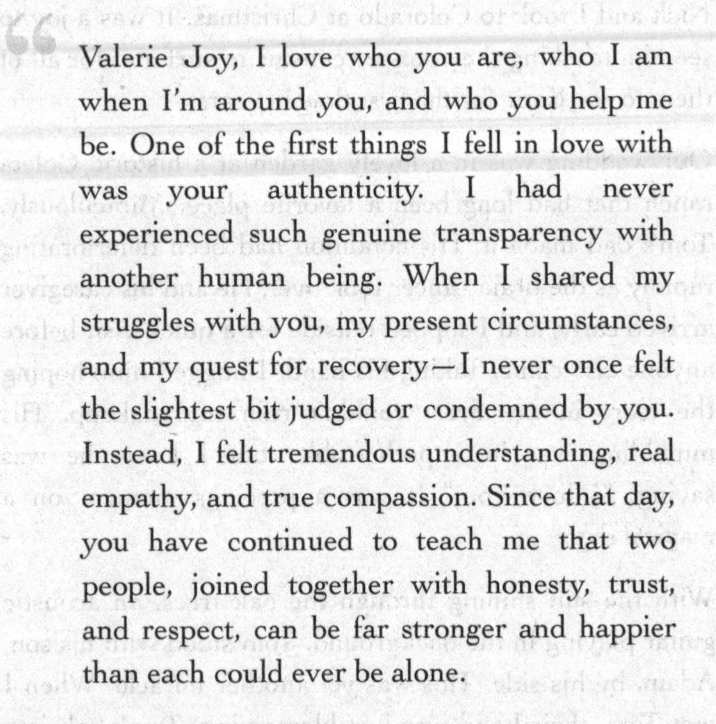

> Valerie Joy, I love who you are, who I am when I'm around you, and who you help me be. One of the first things I fell in love with was your authenticity. I had never experienced such genuine transparency with another human being. When I shared my struggles with you, my present circumstances, and my quest for recovery—I never once felt the slightest bit judged or condemned by you. Instead, I felt tremendous understanding, real empathy, and true compassion. Since that day, you have continued to teach me that two people, joined together with honesty, trust, and respect, can be far stronger and happier than each could ever be alone.

My vows unknowingly mirrored his. With joy in my heart and a sparkle in my eyes, I said,

"I love you because of your depth and emotional intelligence. I love that you are willing to be vulnerable and encourage me to do the same. Our journeys have not always been easy. But we are the people we are today because of the challenges we've faced. When I thought my world was falling apart, it was actually falling into place, and for that, I am truly grateful.

During our casual reception in front of the house, we chatted with our guests, played games on the lawn, and watched the sun set on a beautiful day. I thanked God I hadn't allowed my fear and past failures to keep me from starting over and finding genuine love.

Chapter Twenty-Two

New beginnings are often disguised as painful endings.

Unknown

A few weeks later, we left for an epic two-week honeymoon in Switzerland. The clean air, hiking through the Alps, and exploring a new country was a fantastic experience. We were on top of the world, literally, enjoying our life together. When we returned home, my parents gave us the terrible news that Katie had not been doing well … not just for the weeks we were gone, but for the previous months. She was back to rolling around on the floor, moaning, panting like a menacing wolf, or screaming whenever she was startled. They had waited to tell us how bad it had gotten because they wanted us to enjoy our wedding and honeymoon. But her erratic behaviors were out of control. When she was sleepless, they were sleepless. Her moods held them hostage, and my dad's blood pressure skyrocketed with the stress. One afternoon, my dad texted and asked me to come over because Katie was having another episode. I found her in a highly agitated state and decided to take her to the emergency room. My dad offered to go with me. With her intensity and strength, I feared she'd do something dangerous and welcomed his help.

Bodies filled the waiting room. Because Katie was screaming, sobbing, and disrupting others, we took her outside, and she laid on the ground for several hours while we waited to be seen. When they brought her back to the treatment room, she was crying and yelling, crouched on top of a gurney, like a tiger ready to pounce. Then someone set off the fire alarm, which triggered her further.

She screamed, "Why won't anyone help me? Why won't you help me? Why don't they just kill me?"

The hospital staff sedated her, and dad and I returned home for a few hours. I called every agency under the sun, asking for support. While some crisis response services were available, they all pushed me back to the regional center, which was her primary source of support. Unfortunately, their services focused on intellectual disabilities, not mental health, and their best suggestion was for her to go to the hospital, which wouldn't admit her. So, I refused to sign her out. She was clearly not ready to go home, but the hospital wanted her out of the emergency room. The caseworker threatened to put her out on the street.

I said, "If that's what you need to do, and she gets hurt or hurts someone else, it's on you." She eventually wore me down, and I took her to our house to stay until we could figure something else out.

The familiar tornado was swirling around me. Katie started cutting again, hearing voices, and reported she was blacking out. The psychiatrist suggested she might have borderline personality disorder on top of everything else. Katie cycled through medications like a bored teen swiping through social media. We tried various combinations of mood stabilizers, antipsychotics, antidepressants, and prescriptions for attention deficit disorder. My purpose in life, it seemed, was to keep her alive. But I wanted more for her than this fractured, emotional rollercoaster.

One night, Tom went into Katie's room because he heard her crying.

"Sweetie, what's going on?"

She sobbed, "I just want to be normal."

It was heartbreaking. She was smart enough to know she wasn't typical and yet couldn't overcome it. Tom was compassionate and comforting. He just loved her and listened.

Tom and I never envisioned Katie living with us after our wedding, but it was what needed to happen. Eventually, we fell into a routine that eliminated any stressors for Katie. Coaches came to our home multiple times a week to teach Katie social skills and coping strategies. She had therapy and cooking lessons. It felt like she was healing in our protective, calm bubble. But her life was very small.

Even so, the three of us found our rhythm and did the best we could. I began experiencing the beauty of helping others. Back in the day, I thought I was making a difference in the world by raising money for the parent-teacher association and education foundation, reading books in classrooms, and serving on one board or another. My calendar was filled with these endless activities that filled a request someone had. But anyone could do those things, and I learned years later my perfect facade intimidated people. They didn't share the authentic aspects of their own arduous journeys because they thought I'd judge them. After all, I seemed too perfect. I cringed at the thought I turned people away and missed opportunities to be helpful. But now, I had lots of experience in hard situations and could be helpful as an authentic, recovering perfectionist. It was after the crumbling of the facade that people asked for help.

Will you talk to my friend who has a special needs child struggling in school?

Can you help me set boundaries with my son?

I just need someone to talk with ...

How did you get the school district to pay for residential treatment?

It seemed God put many people in my path at just the right time. I cried in parking lots and at the grocery store as I offered comfort and hope. I followed my gut, the gentle nudging from God, that led me to be available to listen, share my story, and encourage others.

A post on an online blog resonated with me, though the author was unknown.

You are holding a cup of coffee when someone comes along and bumps into you or shakes your arm, making you spill your coffee everywhere.

Why did you spill the coffee?

"Because someone bumped into me!!!"

Wrong answer.

You spilled the coffee because there was coffee in your cup.

Had there been tea in the cup, you would have spilled tea.

Whatever is inside the cup is what will spill out.

Therefore, when life comes along and shakes you (which WILL happen), whatever is inside you will come out. It's easy to fake it until you get rattled.

So we have to ask ourselves … "What's in my cup?"

When life gets tough, what spills over?

Joy, gratefulness, peace, and humility?

Anger, bitterness, harsh words, and reactions?

Life provides the cup. YOU choose how to fill it.

> Today, let's work towards filling our cups with gratitude, forgiveness, joy, words of affirmation, and kindness, gentleness, and love for others.

I wanted goodness and grace to flow from my cup and continued to work on sharing my authentic journey. That Christmas, to encourage those in hard spaces during the season of joy, I wrote a post on social media.

> To the lonely and brokenhearted or those wishing your life differed from what it is, I write this post to say my heart is with you. My Christmas posts haven't always been merry and bright, and on some Christmases, I couldn't write anything.
>
> Not long ago, I was by myself on Christmas Eve, reflecting on years past. It was my first Christmas alone, and I burned letters and pictures from my marriage that had ended. Over the nineteen years of marriage to Paul, there were many "lonely" Christmases with him blacked out and me making excuses for his behavior. Family times were not fun, but we tried to fake it for the kids, who saw through it. I wish I would have had Al-Anon back then because it changed my perspective! Then there were the four Christmases with Katie in a treatment facility. During those years, I wasn't having the picture-perfect

> holidays but felt guilty I didn't feel an ache in my heart because of her absence (and I thought I should if I was a wonderful mom).
>
> I've experienced loss and "less than" holidays. My great expectations have often resulted in sadness and shame. But I know that there is hope for something better. Grace and peace to you in this challenging season.

As the new year began, my focus was on what Katie's next step would be. The previous year, when Katie lived with Paul, he found a program at a California college for young adults with intellectual and developmental disabilities. It sounded like an extraordinary way for Katie to gain life and vocational skill training in a supported environment. Paul and Katie had visited the previous spring, and the program accepted her for the following fall semester. But with the trauma she had experienced with the assault and overdose, we deferred her acceptance so she could heal.

Katie wanted to try again for the upcoming fall, since she had stabilized. My major focus was to help her with that process. We resubmitted her application in January and went to Fresno to re-interview. I was glad to see the campus and student housing since I'd only seen it online and heard Paul's description. She was accepted again, and the entire family felt hopeful.

My mom and I started an Olympic-style training program to prepare Katie. Every day included social skills coaching, cooking lessons, or a shift at the therapeutic riding academy to teach her about volunteering. Her therapist and psychiatrist supported her throughout the process, and we saw her making baby steps of progress.

During these months, Katie also dealt with her feelings about Paul. At first we were all afraid to mention his name in Katie's presence because of her volatile reactions. She would scream if she heard his name. His cards to her went unopened. She hadn't seen or spoken to him since that day in the intensive care unit when she claimed his partner had been emotionally abusive. My communication with him had significantly decreased as well, since we didn't have any parenting coordination. I had no idea where they stood and didn't know if she had the ability to reconcile her feelings. But it wasn't my job to figure it out. Nearly a year after they'd last spoken, Katie told her therapist she was ready and wanted to see Paul again. When I found out, I offered to go with her. But she wanted to do it on her own. They had lunch, and just like that, they had a relationship again.

In July, just as Katie was about to turn twenty years old, Tom and I hosted a college send-off and birthday party with twenty family members, coaches, and friends to celebrate the momentous occasion. I was unsure if Katie could handle it, given the sensory overload and anxiety that came with being the center of attention. During her last party at two years old, she spent most of the time alone in her room. This time, however, she handled her feelings well and announced she was proud of herself. Katie had no filter and would say whatever was on her mind—good or bad, arrogant or insensitive. But that day, she was appropriately excited and emotional as a video of her life played, and people encouraged her on her next adventure.

So many people had helped her along the way, and I was extremely grateful. From the time she arrived in America at sixteen months old, she had therapists of all sorts (play, occupational, adaptive PE, physical, speech, sensory integration, and behavioral), one-on-one aides at school, psychologists, psychiatrists, neurologists, and pediatricians who had cared for her. She had the support of many, including my parents, who had been loving, consistent, and patient in the most trying circumstances. They had stepped in and acted as the primary caregivers at the most challenging times when I could not. I was thankful for their involvement in both of my kids' lives.

I was also grateful for Tom, who jumped into this crazy journey with me. It took an extraordinarily good man to walk willingly into my unpredictable life and embrace it with both arms, a big-hearted sense of humor, and a loving smile. Nick impressed me with his love and support of Katie, too. As I looked around our living room, my heart was full. I was proud of Katie and relieved she would have a path forward and no longer be my daily responsibility. Tom and I were ready to begin our life as empty nesters.

Chapter Twenty-Three

What lies behind you and what lies in front of you pales in comparison to what lies inside of you.

Ralph Waldo Emerson

A week later, with the car crammed full, Katie and I drove the four and a half hours for orientation and check-in. We met her classmates and their parents, and I relished the fact Katie was going to college. She mingled with her new friends while I attended the parent orientation. There were infinite questions for the staff as we prepared to leave our children, the students who we never believed could attend college.

Afterwards, Katie and I finished stocking up on food and supplies for her apartment. She and her three roommates each had their own room and bathroom and shared a tiny kitchen. I was glad I wasn't responsible for instructing them on how to negotiate chores and limited storage space. It was complicated enough for students without disabilities to manage that, let alone those who had trouble navigating the world.

Katie and I unpacked and organized her room, but she was vibrating with excitement and couldn't focus. I let her finish on her own as part of my personal development in surrendering control. I suggested it was time for me to head back home. She was unemotional as we said goodbye, and I knew she would not miss me. She was simply excited to open a new chapter.

A few days later, I called but got Katie's voice mail. Soon after, a text appeared.

"I'll text you later. I'm with my friends right now."

"I meant to text you yesterday, but I got caught up in the pool party."

That Katie was doing something social was remarkable. She had never had many friends, and the fact she was establishing relationships was welcome news. But the honeymoon phase passed quickly. It began with Katie verbally lashing out and not completing her homework and chores. It escalated to crying and shouting in her bedroom at all hours. Her behavior surprised the program staff, but not me. This was how it had always been. She could hold it together for some amount of time and later melted down. The pages and pages in Katie's application documented this pattern. When I spoke with Katie about it before she left for school, she said she was determined to make it work this time.

Because the staff worked with students with intellectual

disabilities, not those with mental health issues, they didn't know how to respond and reached out to me for advice.

I said, "Have you helped her set up the therapy appointment yet?"

"No, we haven't gotten to it. It's been so busy with the beginning of the year," her case manager replied.

"She really needs to get to therapy ASAP. Do you know if she's been taking her medication?" I asked.

"No, we don't monitor medication."

"I realize that, but when I met with you at check-in, I was explicit about how critical these are for her well-being. She needs therapy, so she doesn't lose all the progress she's made. We did the initial set up over the summer. She just needs you or one of your team to help her make the call," I replied.

At home, Katie and I had done everything we could to set her up for success. She set medication reminders on her phone. She had access to limited amounts of her medication, given her previous suicide attempt, and took it without us prompting her. Katie practiced making appointments with her social skills coach. But the therapist's office would not schedule her until she was in Fresno. She needed the program staff to help her with the call because her speech was difficult to understand when she was flustered or anxious.

It took all of my self-restrain to remain calm. It was no surprise she wasn't doing well. If she wasn't taking her prescriptions or taking part in weekly therapy, she would fall apart.

I called Katie and discussed her actions and program participation. To stay in school, she needed to follow their rules and behavioral standards. If she didn't, they could kick her out. She seemed to understand.

The staff continued to coach Katie on her classwork and life skills, and how to get along with her peers. They called me when she was not compliant, and I again inquired about whether the in-home support staff had asked Katie about the medication or helped her make the therapy appointment. The answer was still no.

It was infuriating because the solution to the problem seemed so straightforward. I felt helpless being so far away. I called and texted Katie. She said she was taking care of it, but it seemed she was lying because her behaviors weren't improving.

One afternoon, the Federal Bureau of Investigation (FBI) contacted Paul and me. Katie had tweeted something that could be interpreted as a threat to people who didn't support the LGBTQ lifestyle. The agent and I spoke about whether Katie had the means and capacity to harm others. I was certain she did not. But he needed to speak to Katie, and I agreed to prepare her for his call, since she wouldn't answer an unknown number.

After I hung up with the agent, awful thoughts rolled around in my mind. *Did Katie have the ability to do something terrible? Her staff described behaviors while at her treatment centers that I wouldn't have expected. Was I missing something … anything?* I didn't want to be one of those mothers who felt something was off but did nothing to protect others from their murderer child.

I called Katie after a few minutes.

"Katie, an FBI agent wants to speak to you about something you tweeted," I said.

"Okay."

"What did you tweet?"

"I don't know."

"How can you not know? What's your Twitter name so I can look it up?"

"I don't have a Twitter account," she replied.

"The FBI thinks you do."

Then I realized I assumed this was recent.

"Have you ever had a Twitter account?"

"Yeah, but that was like last year," she said.

She couldn't recall what she had written, and no longer knew her Twitter login. I searched and discovered nothing, so I let the process play out. Katie spoke to the agent but couldn't relay their conversation to me. He never contacted me again, and the FBI didn't storm her apartment, so I guessed they didn't consider her a threat. It was yet another thing I never expected in motherhood.

One month into the program, the students gave a progress report to their parents and the staff. I dreaded what I would hear. Usually the group met in person, but because I lived four and a half hours away and had already been there four times that year, I said it would have to be a conference call. I also considered if I was there, they might make me take her home that day.

Paul and I both called in and listened as Katie provided a positive report. He and I texted in disbelief that Katie thought things were going well. *Was she manipulating us because we weren't there? Did she think that if she was positive, then we would somehow believe it was true? Who was she trying to impress?*

When the staff presented their part of the report, they shared several disturbing incidents. One time, Katie screamed during a video on sexual violence and yelled at a peer who was startled by her outburst. Katie explained the presentation triggered her because of past experiences and expressed remorse. Katie had also started carrying a chef's knife in her backpack because she felt safer with it. The staff asked her how they could be supportive, but also made it clear she could not remain if her behavior didn't change. Katie said she understood and would try harder. She promised to ask staff for help in the future.

If she was ever going to function independently, this was the best chance. She was supposed to be learning the skills necessary to maintain an apartment, set a budget, plan and prepare meals, shop for groceries, and pay rent. The vocational component provided work experience and an internship to help students transition back into their local community and have a productive and fulfilling life. I struggled to not overthink the future and the fact she might be kicked out. My daily personal pep talk was "She's not getting kicked out today."

However, one Friday night, about six weeks after I'd dropped her off and two weeks after the parent conference, it became apparent her time was up. I received numerous calls from her staff over several hours. She threatened one of her roommates with a knife and screamed at another. Then she locked herself in her room and yelled and sobbed intermittently for several hours. It terrified her roommates, and the staff didn't know what to do. When they called me, I said it sounded like Katie needed to go to the emergency room for a psychiatric hold

I called Katie.

"Hi." Katie's voice was meek.

"Hi. What's going on?" I said in the calmest voice I could muster, even though I was furious.

"I don't know"

"You obviously do know. I'm hearing you have been screaming and crying for several hours and that you won't talk to your staff."

"Yeah."

"And at some point you had your head in the oven?" I asked.

"Yeah."

"Why would you do that?"

"I don't know."

"Will you please talk to your staff?"

"They can't help me. No one can help me," she shrieked.

A flood of tears, sniffling, and nose-blowing followed. I wanted to scream in frustration. She was destroying her future. I waited on the line for what seemed like an hour.

She said, "I hope I see you again."

"That's a crappy thing to say to your mother," I replied. I felt weary. We'd been through this so many times before.

I continued, "It's your choice. I hope I get to see you, but if you decide otherwise, I'll be sad."

"I know. I love you," Katie said.

"I love you, too."

And I hung up, not knowing if that would be the last time we spoke.

The police arrived for a welfare check and called an ambulance. It took a while for the officers to coax her out of her room. They handcuffed her because of her aggressive behavior and took her to the emergency room. I called Paul and my parents to update them. All of us were heartbroken, but not surprised.

A nurse contacted me to verify her diagnoses and insurance information but provided few details about how Katie was doing. The program staff called me from the hospital. They had never handled a psychiatric hold, and I had to walk them through the process instead of receiving the support I desperately needed. Tom and I discussed me going there, but decided there wasn't any benefit. Katie would not find comfort with me there.

The most challenging part was figuring out how to care for myself that evening. I couldn't let fear and strain overtake me. My body couldn't tolerate the impact stress had on my blood sugars. While I had become very proficient at managing my diabetes, these types of incidents made the disease feel unmanageable. It felt selfish, but I had learned that I had to take care of myself so I could tend to her.

My journey always felt so lonely because there wasn't a roadmap or handbook for parenting kids with Katie's unique combination of needs. There were groups for parents of autistic children or those with reactive attachment disorder or with mental health issues, but not all three. I knew other parents had much more severe conditions they were dealing with, but it didn't make me feel better.

The hospital kept Katie for several days and then transferred her to a psychiatric facility in San Francisco, the only one that would take someone with her diagnoses. She stayed for several weeks, heavily medicated. Because she was legally an adult, they wouldn't give me much information and only contacted me about the payment and discharge planning.

While she was there, Tom and I drove the four and a half hours to clean out her apartment and turn over the keys. Her room and bathroom reeked of her decline. They were filthy, and it was obvious she wasn't well. Food and trash littered her floor, and her school supplies sat unopened. The refrigerator held her moldy produce and expired milk. I wondered what she had been doing the last six weeks and whether she eaten anything other than candy. It was one of the longest days of my life, driving there and back, filled with grief at yet another disappointment for Katie.

I couldn't believe I had been so optimistic. Maybe optimistic wasn't the right word. Maybe I was clinging to hope and ignoring the voice in my head that knew how unlikely it would be for her to succeed. The pattern was apparent. It felt like all the therapy, time, money, energy, and prayer hadn't made a difference.

I was defeated. There was no supported living environment for people like Katie, unless you could afford the $12,000 per month price tag. On a societal level, it puzzled me. Katie was eligible for hours and hours of coaching with sweet college-aged girls who worked on conversation and emotional stability. Unfortunately, Katie could only apply those skills in a hyper-managed environment with no stress or pressure. The state's Employment Development Department would assist her in exploring and finding a career which she couldn't pursue because her mental health dictated her function. Social security denied her disability claim twice because Katie charmed the evaluator and appeared to have great potential. But the mounds of evidence proved otherwise. Her reactive attachment disorder allowed her to fool most people, except those who had lived with her. Katie could hold it together for a while—until she couldn't.

Chapter Twenty-Four

Even the darkest night will end, and the sun will rise.

Victor Hugo, *Les Misérables*

When it became clear Katie was headed toward another disastrous meltdown, I found a therapist specializing in helping families of loved ones with mental illness. I needed support and, now that Tom was intertwined with me on this parenting experience, I wanted him to understand how to help me as well. Tom and I knew we couldn't go back to the way it was. We had agreed to have her with us for a short time, because living with Paul was not an option. When she was stable, it wasn't difficult, but her presence was like a black cloud hovering over us. I didn't want to give up our peaceful life and return to that environment.

During one of our therapy appointments, two things were weighing heavily—my reluctance to continue as Katie's case manager and feeling pressured by the hospital and the agency responsible for her care, to come up with a solution to the question of what was next for Katie. As we discussed it, the therapist said that I didn't have to be the solution. I was shocked. I didn't know I could say I wasn't comfortable or able to have her in my home and did not know I didn't have to be her case manager. Katie had an assigned case manager at the social service agency, and she would have to figure it out without my help. It was as if a switch flipped. The concept that I didn't have to do their jobs for them because I was the parent was unbelievable. The therapist said it was typical for agencies to push parents to be the caregivers without conveying other options available.

I couldn't believe I no longer had to be in charge of Katie and could still be a good mom. He asked what I needed to feel comfortable to make those changes. I said I needed Nick to believe I had done my best with Katie. We talked through that for a while. When Tom and I left, I felt empowered to leave my old roles behind. Instead of engaging in the placement games between the hospital and the regional center case manager, I pushed back and encouraged them to collaborate. I wrote a strong email to Katie's case manager, citing legal authority that allowed the regional center the ability to provide supportive housing for Katie. It was thrilling to feel like I was taking back control of my life while advocating for Katie.

Feeling emboldened, I updated Nick on what was happening. Since he lived on his own, he hadn't seen Katie since her launch party and didn't know about her transition and meltdown. I hated telling him because there was nothing he could do and, like always, I wanted to protect him from the truth.

Later on, I learned that keeping secrets and not being honest was typical in an alcoholic household. While I hadn't grown up with it, I realized I'd lived with it in my marriage almost as long as I'd lived with my parents. I never thought about my marriage negatively impacting my thought patterns—and why would I? My only model for marriage had been a healthy and stable one.

When I told Nick about Katie, he was sad for her but empathetic toward me.

He said, "Mom, you have done everything a mother can do and more. No one could have done what you've done. She needs to do her part, too."

Tears rolled down my face, and I could barely speak. It was as if Nick had overheard the conversation with my therapist and said exactly what I needed.

When he was struggling during high school, he couldn't understand why I wouldn't give up on him. I told him that was what moms do ... we rally around our children. And while I wasn't giving up on Katie, there was nothing further I could do.

After we hung up, I thought about Katie's journey. In retrospect, it was so presumptuous and naïve to think Paul and I could give this girl a wonderful life. From conception, she was at a disadvantage because of the alcohol and drugs her birth mother used. No amount of therapy, love, nourishment, and medical care could overcome those tragic beginnings. But I didn't know that as I relentlessly sought answers to unanswerable questions. My unwavering faith in God led to the delusional optimism that He would heal her so her life would be better. But He chose not to, for whatever reason, and I had to trust that there was something about this plan for her life that I couldn't understand.

Each time Katie made progress, I held my breath, hoping it would be the time something finally clicked. Yet, each time she stumbled, sometimes to the edge of her life, I wasn't surprised. I finally accepted I had to let go. The control I thought I had wasn't helping Katie and was hurting me. I had to get off the rollercoaster. I had to once again look forward and trust that God had her in his palm, without my hand in between.

While Katie was sitting in a hospital bed in San Francisco, waiting for someone to come up with a discharge plan, I attended a job-related workshop. The presenter spoke about traumatic experiences and the cumulative effect they had. I thought about Katie's adverse childhood impacts, or ACEs as they are called in the educational realm, and then the traumatic experiences in my life. The diabetes diagnoses. The diabetic kidney disease and being told I would never have children because of it. Miscarrying two babies. Katie's ever-changing list of serious diagnoses. Sending her to multiple long-term locked treatment facilities. Hearing a peer had molested her. Hearing she'd been sexually assaulted again. Going through multiple suicide attempts with my children. Realizing my husband was an alcoholic, and gay. Being told each of my parents had cancer. The list went on. These experiences, sometimes in rapid succession, were gut-wrenching. I developed a thick scar on my heart I thought would protect me, but instead it prevented me from learning the lessons I needed: Life has no script or formula. There is more to life than perfection. I have the power to forge my own path, trusting God will guide me.

I wish I had known these things earlier, rather than suffering all those years. I realized looking perfect on the outside was my way of distracting myself from the true me. It made me feel in control, so I didn't have to handle all the challenging emotions I didn't feel safe expressing. The only difference between my perfectionist self-harm and Katie's cutting was that I wore mine like a badge of honor—as if perfection was something to be revered. The facade was my protective armor. As long as I was harder on myself than anyone else, no one could hurt me. What if, instead of striving for perfection, I had known there was something better?

I learned a lot about myself over those traumatic years and found healing. I came to believe marrying Paul wasn't a bad decision. I had done the best I could with the information I had at the time. I wouldn't have my life, my story, and my children without him. I accepted my childhood the way it was because I believed they had done the best they could. They were my parents, and I loved them. They were tremendous grandparents to my children. Nick, in particular, would not be the person he was and have the job he did, without the consistent, positive influence and time with my dad.

Because of my individual struggles, as well as the ones we had together, my relationship with my parents had become more authentic. And my mom finally told me the things I needed to hear from her. This past Mother's Day, she said, "You have been just what Nick and Katie needed. Find joy in Nick's growth and Katie's stability. I love you and I'm proud of the person you are."

I had also found my path and a peace and freedom in experiencing God, the one I met when I took time to discover Him for myself. I no longer feared his judgment and woke up every day filled with gratitude and optimism.

If I hadn't gone through those traumatic experiences, I wouldn't be the person I am today. It sounds so simplistic. If my life and marriage had worked out according to my script, I wouldn't have this wonderfully imperfect life, living with joy, in spite of the hardships. I am a changed person. Instead of being judgmental and competitive, I try to be gracious, good-hearted, and helpful. And my relationship with God, the God of my understanding, is much richer as a result of my struggles.

One of the beautiful parts of my life was seeing the broken pieces fit together in unexpected ways. Before I met Tom, his disease prevented him from being fully present for his son's early years. However, a gift of his sobriety was the development of a more secure relationship, which I got to witness in its early stages when Tom and I started dating. It was breathtaking to see the beauty rising from the broken.

Similarly, I saw it with Nick and Paul. On one of Nick's birthdays, Tom and I took him to dinner, and I asked if he'd done anything with his dad to celebrate, not knowing where their relationship stood.

He said, "Yeah, Paul texted me and asked me to have lunch, so I went. I figured if he was going to have real interest in me, I'd go because he will always be my dad."

After the divorce, I tried not to speak badly about Paul because, like Nick said, he would always be the kids' dad, and I had seen how Paul's troubled relationship with his father affected him. I always told Nick I hoped they would reconcile because resentments only hurt the person doing the resenting, something I wished I'd learned earlier. So, the fact he understood this at twenty-one years old was amazing.

Stepping back, I could see how the broken pieces of my life had created an exquisite mosaic. God had blessed me with an imperfect life so I could find the one I was meant to have.

Epilogue

The hospital in San Francisco released Katie from the psychiatric hold after three weeks. They called an Uber, which transported her three hundred miles from San Francisco to a temporary group home in Santa Barbara. Six weeks later, she plead her case for permanent disability wearing her tattered sweatshirt and faded yoga pants, accompanied by her attorney and her stuffed animal, Steve. After two years of fighting for this critical support, the judge decided in Katie's favor within ten minutes. The Social Security Administration challenged Katie's immigration status before it would begin making disability payments, but that eventually got resolved with the help of our congressional representative's office.

Katie currently lives in a group home in southern California and has not been on a psychiatric hold for two years. She's become a talented artist and displays her work on Instagram to diminish the stigma of those living with autism, depression, anxiety, and reactive attachment disorder. She recently texted and said, "Thank you, Mom, for taking care of me. I forgive you. You are my role model and everything I learned, I learned from you. Love you." I am grateful for her stability and self-awareness.

Nick is happy, healthy, and living his dream in Santa Cruz. He surfs as much as possible while excelling at his day job in construction. Each year on Mother's Day, I remember back to where we were and thank God for Nick's transformation.

Tom and I strive to become better versions of ourselves daily and help others in any way we can. We embrace each adventure that comes our way and are thankful our paths intersected so we could live our extraordinary life together.

A note to those experiencing difficult times: I would not have the life I have today, filled with love and joy, without the difficult parts of my journey. I want to encourage you that you can get through tough times, too. Be strong. Rise above. And choose your own adventure.

Grateful Acknowledgements

Thank you to everyone who believed I had a story to tell and could articulate it well. On this writing journey, I'm particularly grateful for the encouragement and feedback from Chrisanna, Yvonne, Anita, Dianne, Karen, and Robynne

Thank you to those individuals who have filled my soul over the years—Kristen, Chrisanna, and my Westmont crew—Kelly, Jen, and Shannon—you are treasures.

Nick and Katie, thank you for forgiving me for the things I could have done better and for your support in sharing my story. I'm tremendously grateful you are thriving and am blessed to be your mom.

Adam, you are the best bonus child I could ask for. I'm grateful for our authentic connection.

Mom and Dad, thank you for being terrific grandparents and giving servants, and for working through the messy parts of life with me.

To my knight in rusty armor, Tom, thank you for believing in me, being a hopeless romantic, and encouraging me to shine. You are the best part of my rescripted life. I love you with all my heart and look forward to finding more heart rocks on our adventures.

Endnotes

Chapter 1. Unknown

Chapter 2. Isaiah 43:2 (New Living Translation)

Chapter 3. Saint Augustine. Source: Unknown

Chapter 4. Excerpt from *Jesus Calling* by Sarah Young.

Copyright © 2004-10-10 by Sarah Young. Used by permission of Thomas Nelson. www.thomasnelson.com

Chapter 5. Laura Ingalls Wilder. Source: "A Bouquet of Wild Flowers," article published in the Missouri Ruralist. July 20, 1917

Chapter 6. John Maxwell. Source: Instagram @myBible

Chapter 7. Jean-Paul Sartre. Source: Essay

Chapter 8. John Piper. Source: www.desiringgod.org/embrace-the-life-god-has-given-you

Chapter 9. Voyage of the Dawn Treader (film). Screenwriters Christopher Markus, Stephen McFeely, and Michael Petroni

Chapter 10. Used with permissions from Fi Newood

Chapter 11. Excerpt from *For the Love* by Jen Hatmaker. Copyright © 2018-04-10 by Jen Hatmaker. Used by permission of Thomas Nelson. www.thomasnelson.com

Chapter 12. Joseph Campbell. Source: *Excerpt from Reflections on the Art of Living: A Joseph Campbell Companion*, Selected and edited by Diane K. Osbon. HarperCollins

Chapter 13. Paulo Cohelo. Source: Paulo Coelho's Facebook page

Chapter 14. Jen Hatmaker. Excerpt from *Of Mess and Moxie* by Jen Hatmaker. Copyright © 2017-08-08 by Jen Hatmaker. Used by permission of Thomas Nelson. www.thomasnelson.com

Chapter 15. Helen Keller. Source: Handwritten in a document housed by the American Federation for the Blind and attributed to Helen Keller

Chapter 16. Eleanor Roosevelt. Source: www.fdrlibrary.org/eleanor-roosevelt

Chapter 17. Brené Brown.
Source: May 24, 2018 blog post at brenebrown.com

Chapter 18. Unknown

Chapter 19. Suzanne Stabile. Source: Instagram @suzannestabile

Chapter 20. Unknown

Chapter 21. Karen Casey. Excerpt from *Each Day a New Beginning: A Meditation Book and Journal for Daily Reflection* by Karen Casey. Copyright @ April 19, 2001. Published by Hazelden Publishing.

Chapter 22. Unknown

Chapter 23. Attributed to Ralph Waldo Emerson (unverified)

Chapter 24. Victor Hugo, *Les Misérables*

Resources

Be strong enough to face the world each day.
Be weak enough to know you cannot do everything alone.

Unknown

Al-Anon Family Groups (Al-Anon)

Al-Anon.org

Al-Anon is a program for loved ones of those with a drinking problem, although it is useful for any type of addiction. Al-Anon groups meet in over 130 countries to help families and friends of problem drinkers recover from the impacts of a loved one's drinking. Members help each other by practicing the Twelve Steps of Alcoholics Anonymous themselves, by welcoming and comforting families of alcoholics, and by giving understanding and encouragement to the alcoholic.

National Alliance of Mental Illness (NAMI)

www.nami.org

NAMI's Family-to-Family program is extremely helpful for parents, spouses, children, and loved ones of those with mental illness. It is a free, eight-session educational, evidence-based program taught by trained NAMI members. The classes include presentations, discussions, and interactive exercises, and participants find support with others facing similar difficult situations.

National Association of Therapeutic Schools and Programs (NATSAP)

www.natsap.org

NATSAP is the largest not-for-profit membership association in the United States dedicated to residential treatment centers, therapeutic board schools, and wilderness therapy programs. It is an advocate and resource for organizations that devote themselves to the need for the effective care and education of struggling young people and their families.

Note: Because of the ever-changing nature of the Internet, web addresses may change after the time of publication.

About the Author

Valerie Cantella's love of writing began when her stubby fingers learned to form letters, and those letters became words that crafted sentences. From those sentences, she wrote short stories, articles, and poems, and a book for her grade school author showcase. She turned to journalism and a career in communications and now works as a public affairs and communication consultant.

Valerie has three children, a biological son, an adopted daughter, and a bonus son by marriage. She lives in Santa Barbara, CA, with her husband Tom, and volunteers with organizations where she can use her experience to help others.

I will look forward. I will trust God. Today is a new day.

Connect with Valerie on Instagram @valeriejcantella

www.ValerieCantella.com

CPSIA information can be obtained
at www.ICGtesting.com
Printed in the USA
LVHW101322140322
713357LV00022B/732